TOTALLY RADICAL SPORTS

&

GIRLS PLAYING SPORTS

COLORING BOOK

Totally Radical SPORTS Coloring Book

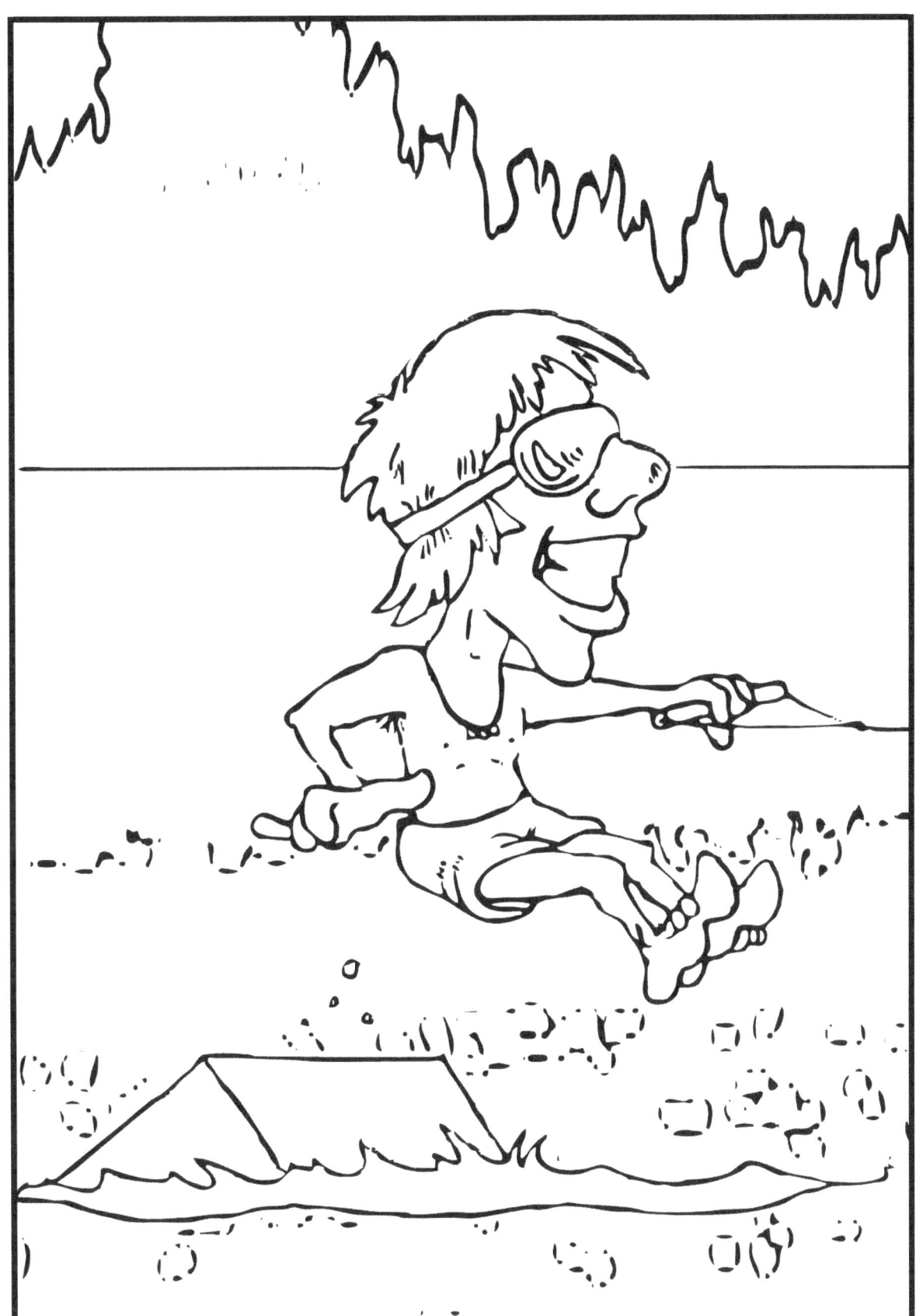

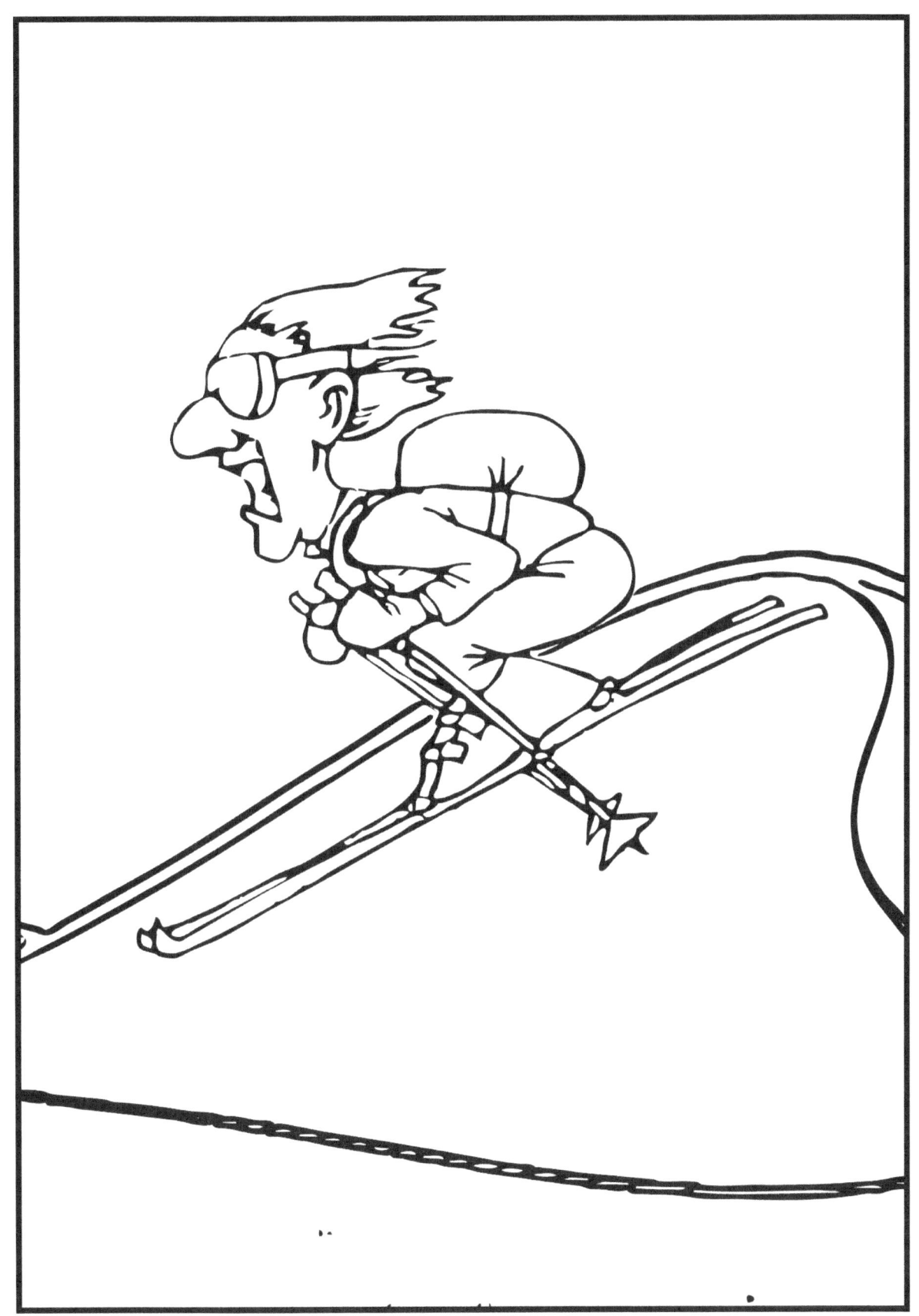

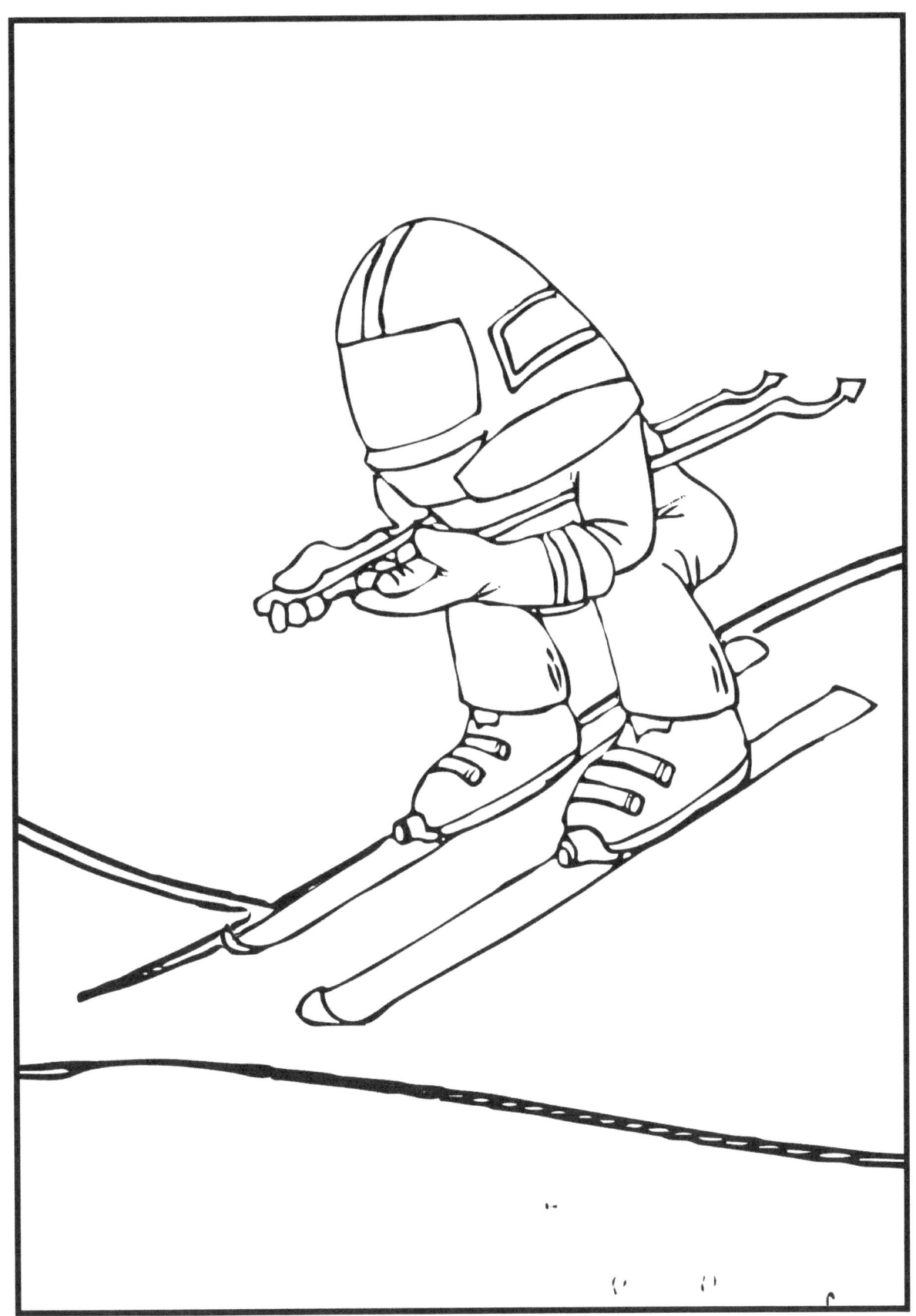

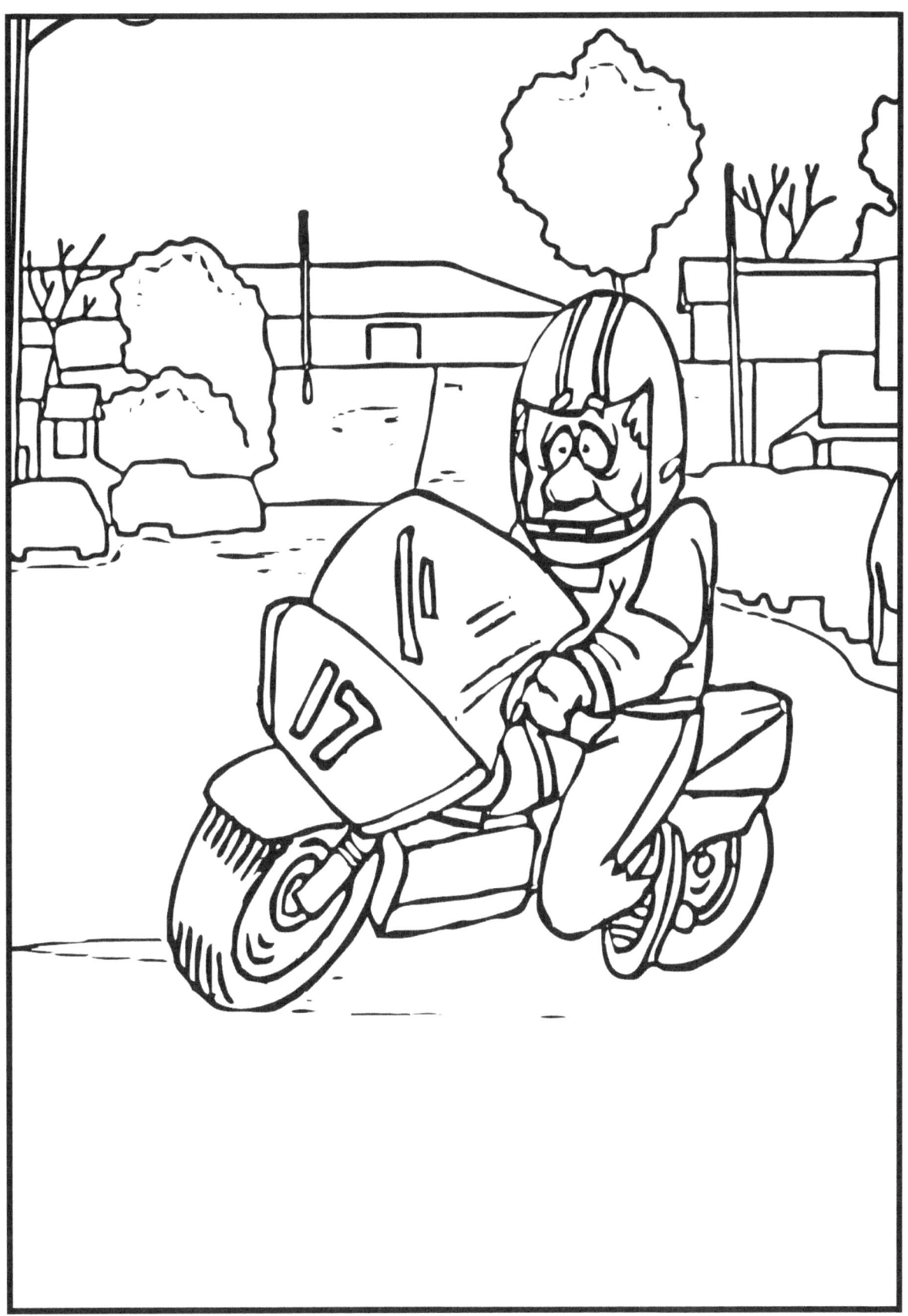

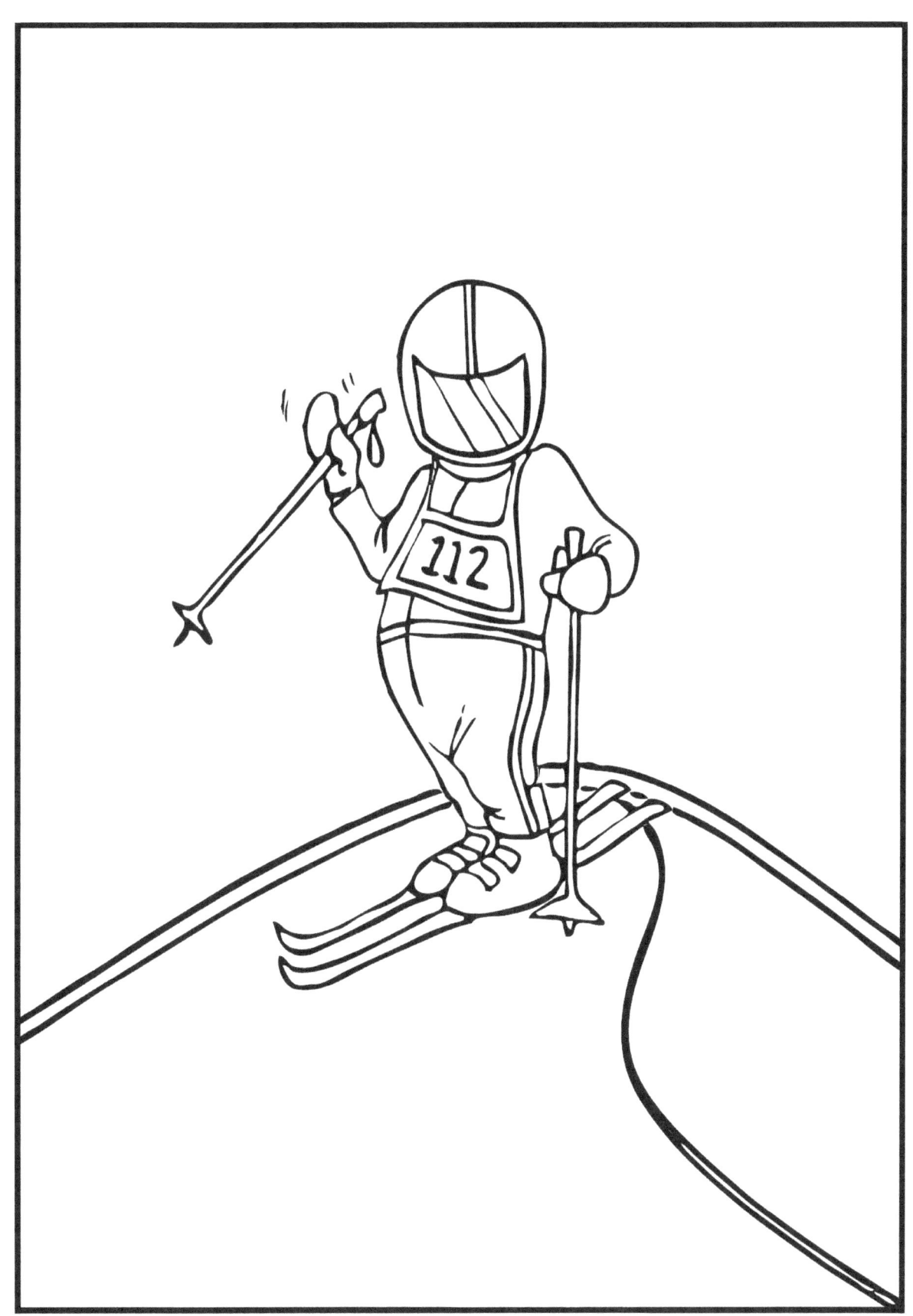

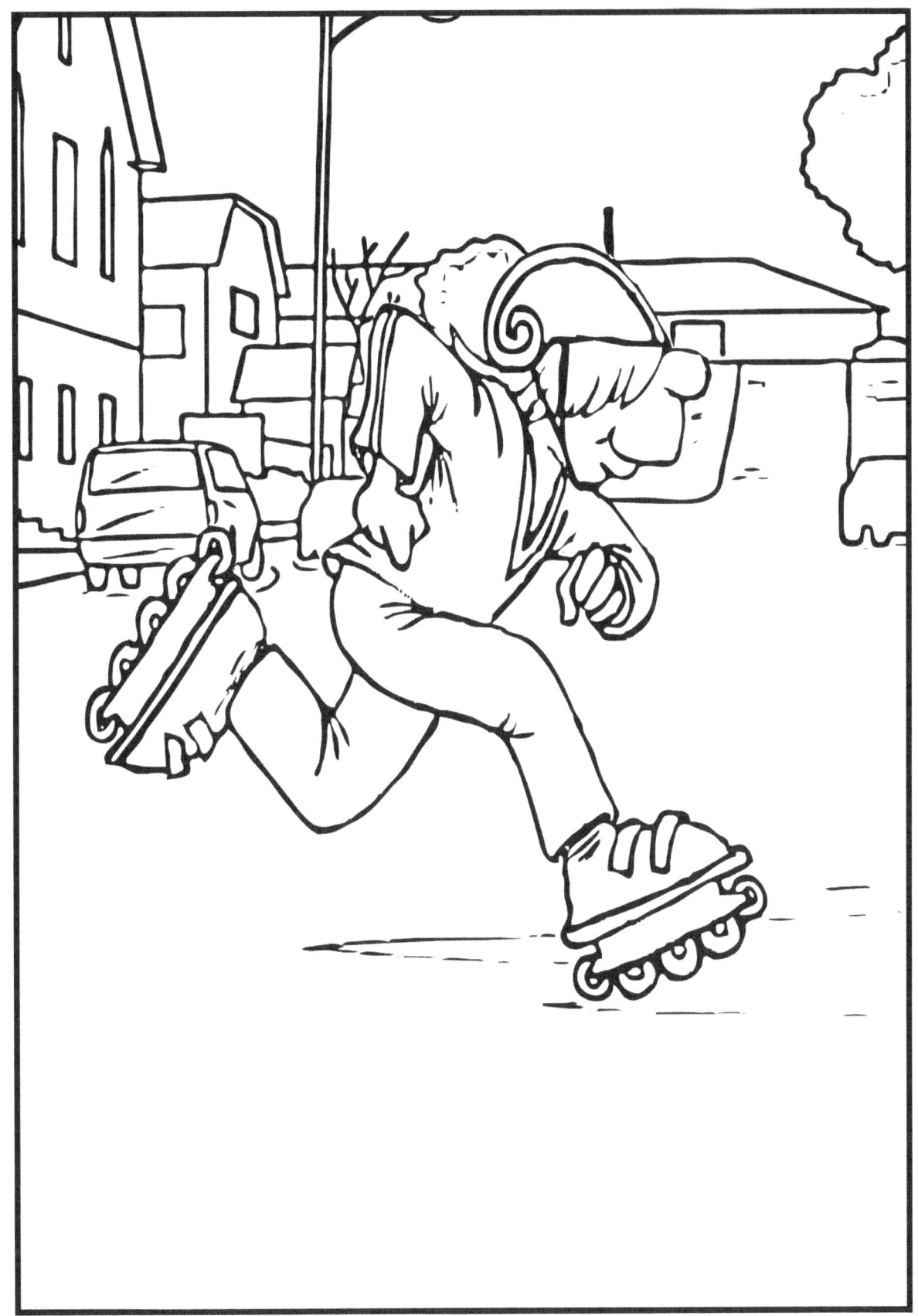

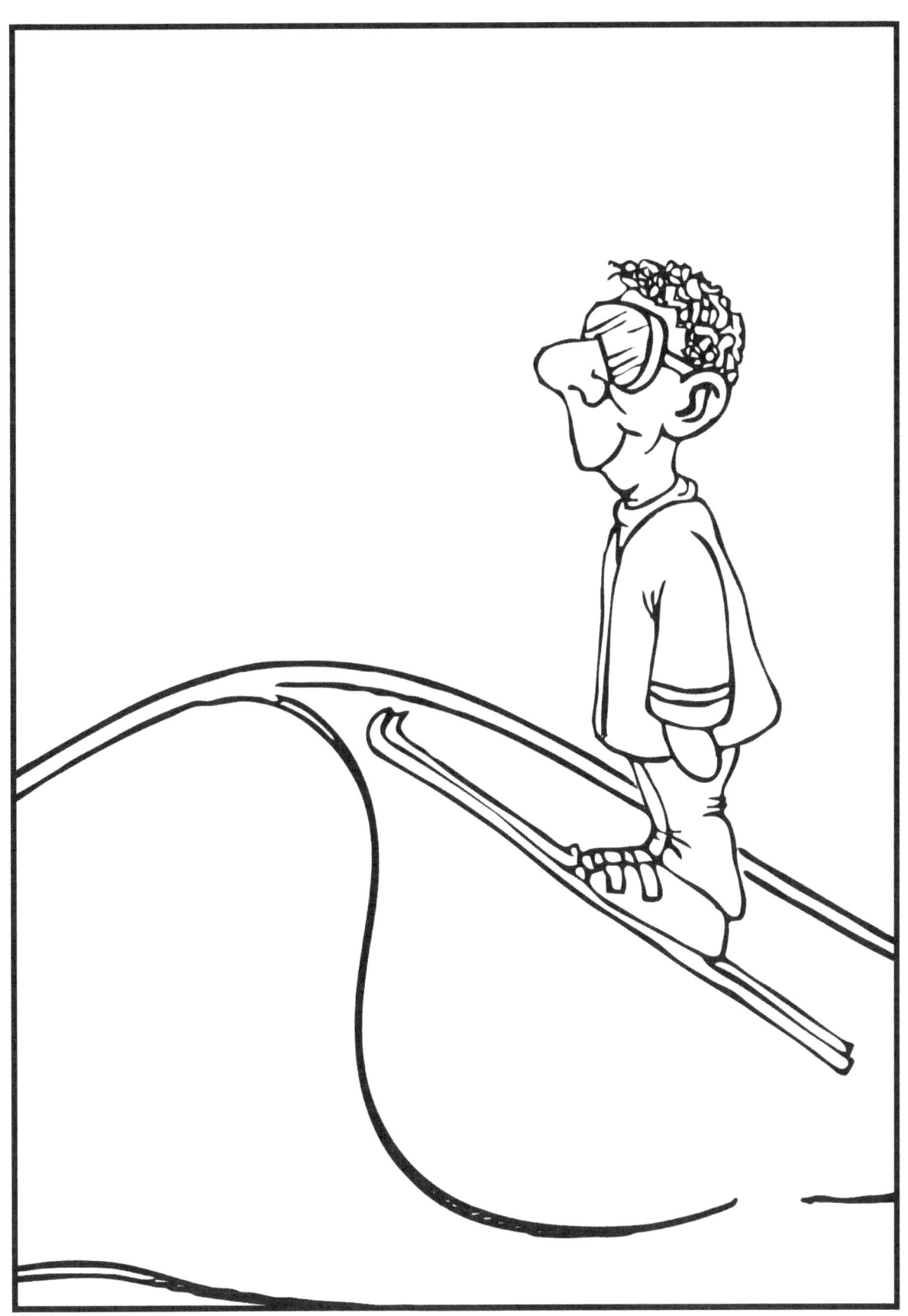

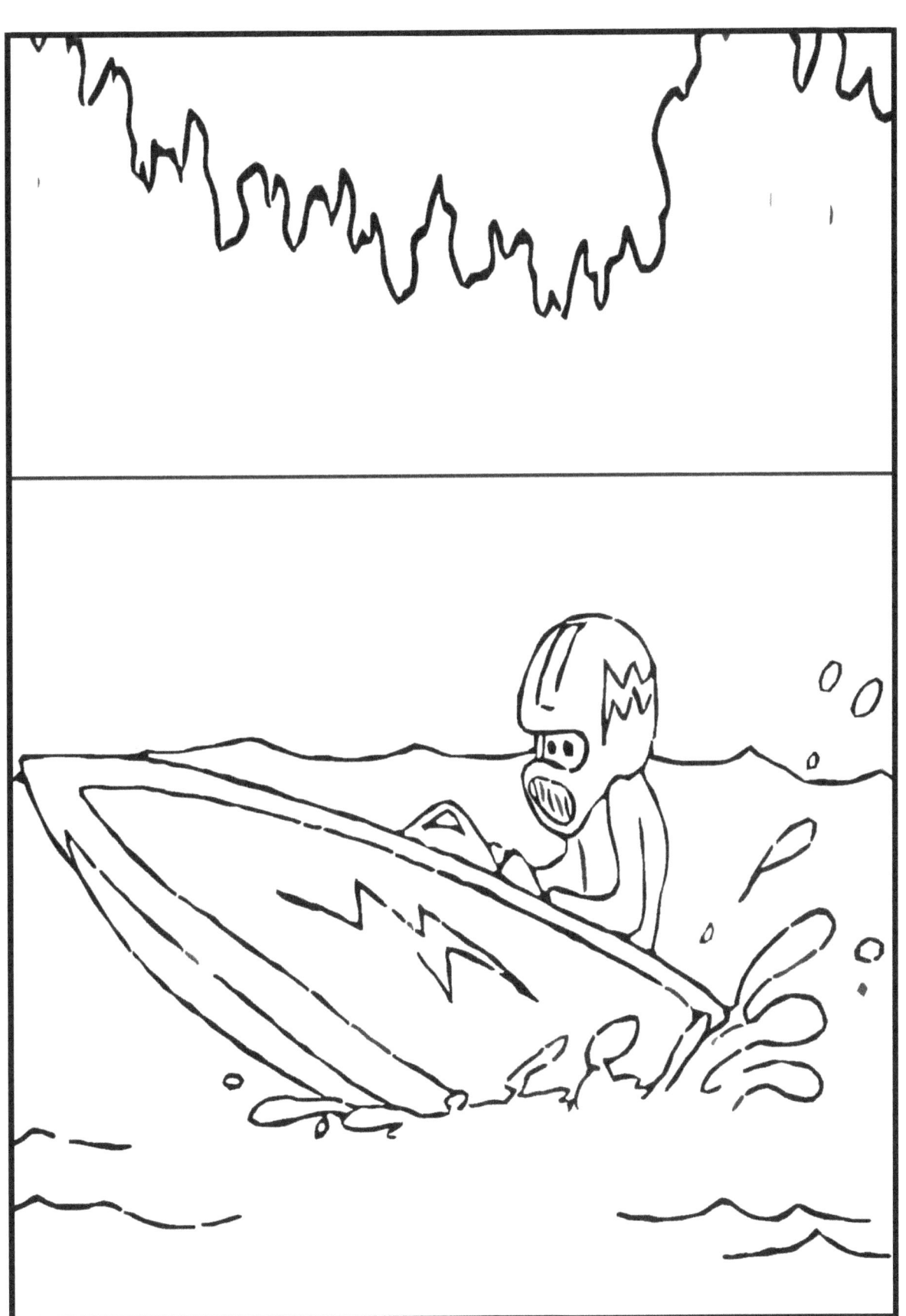

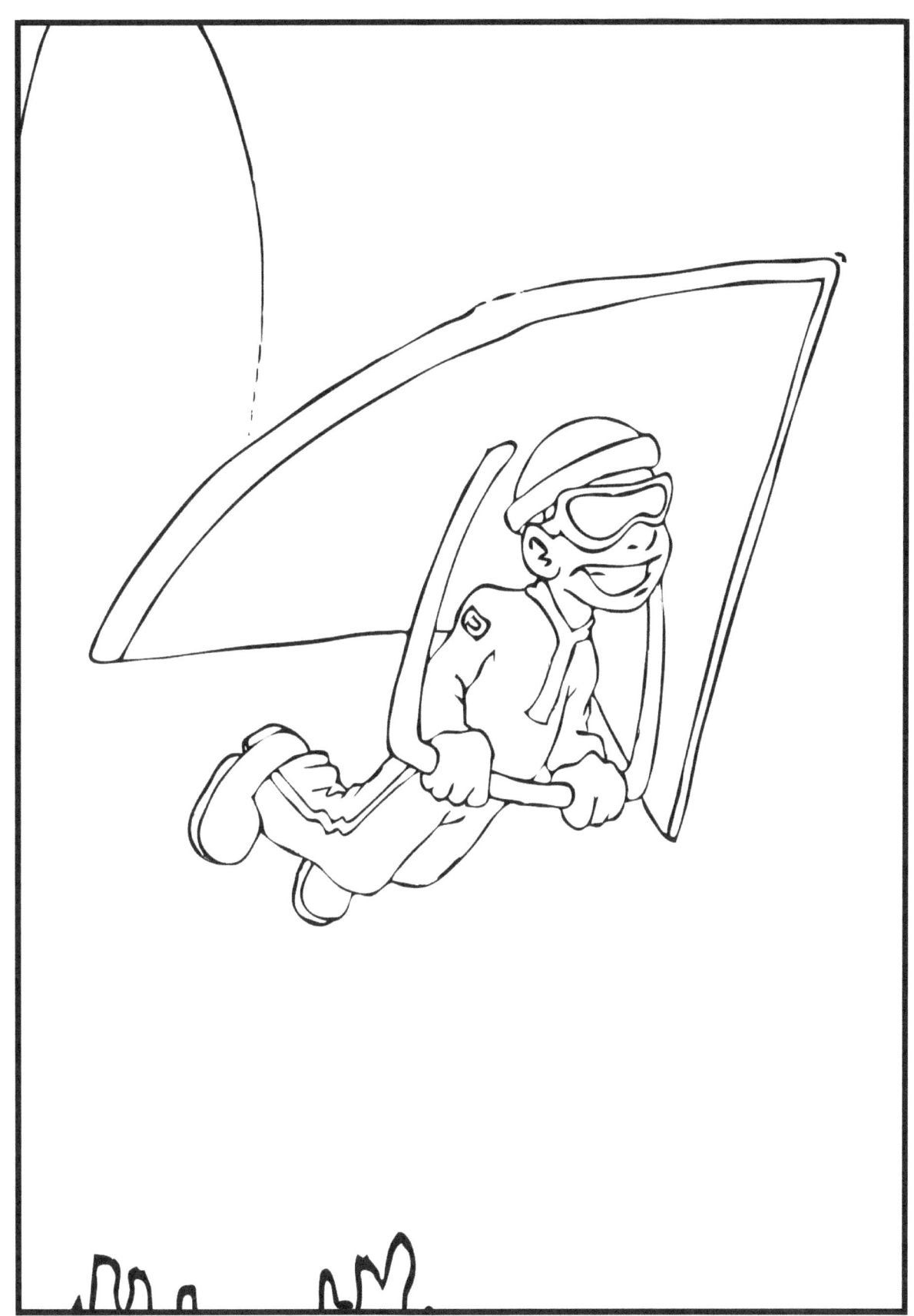

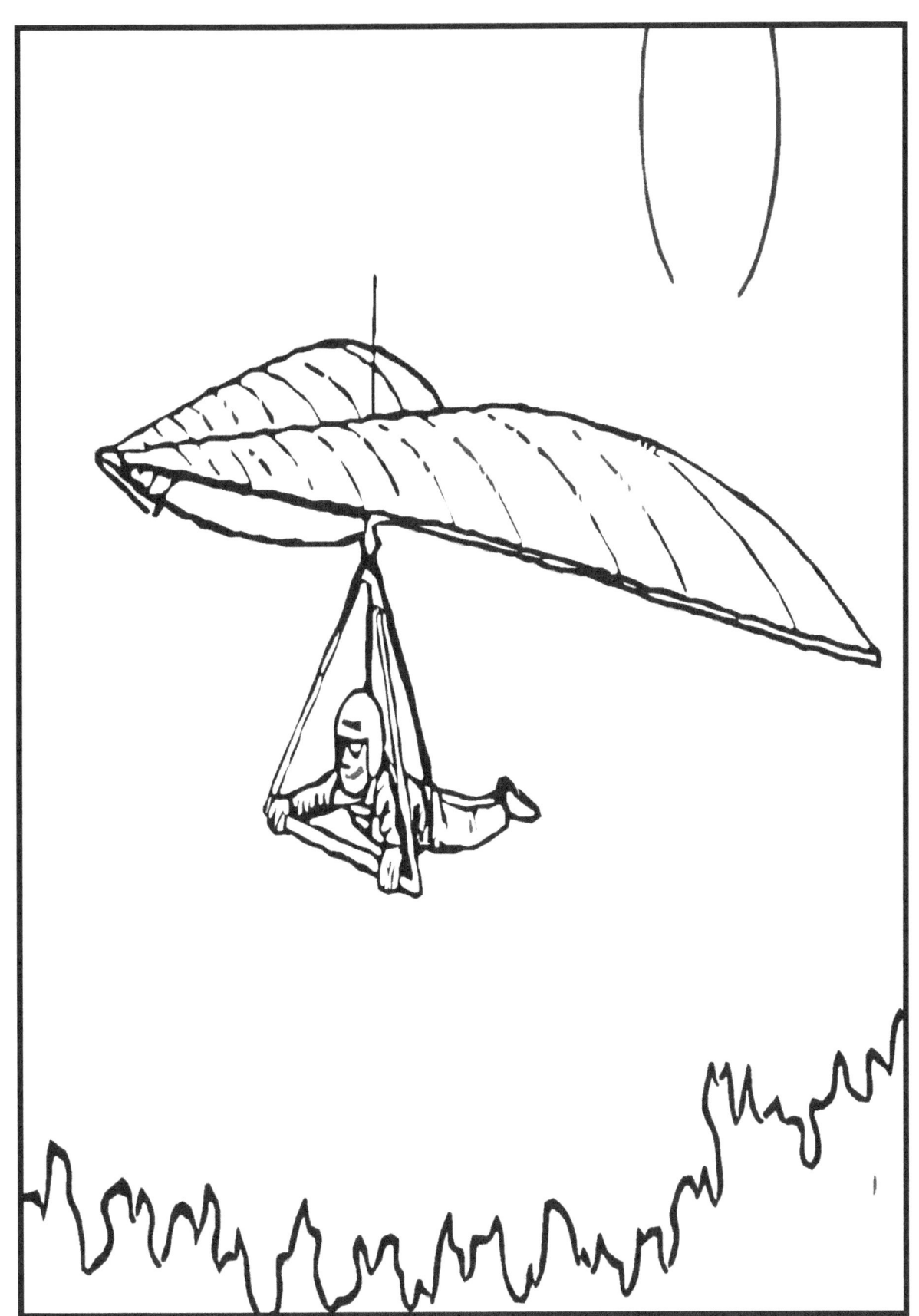

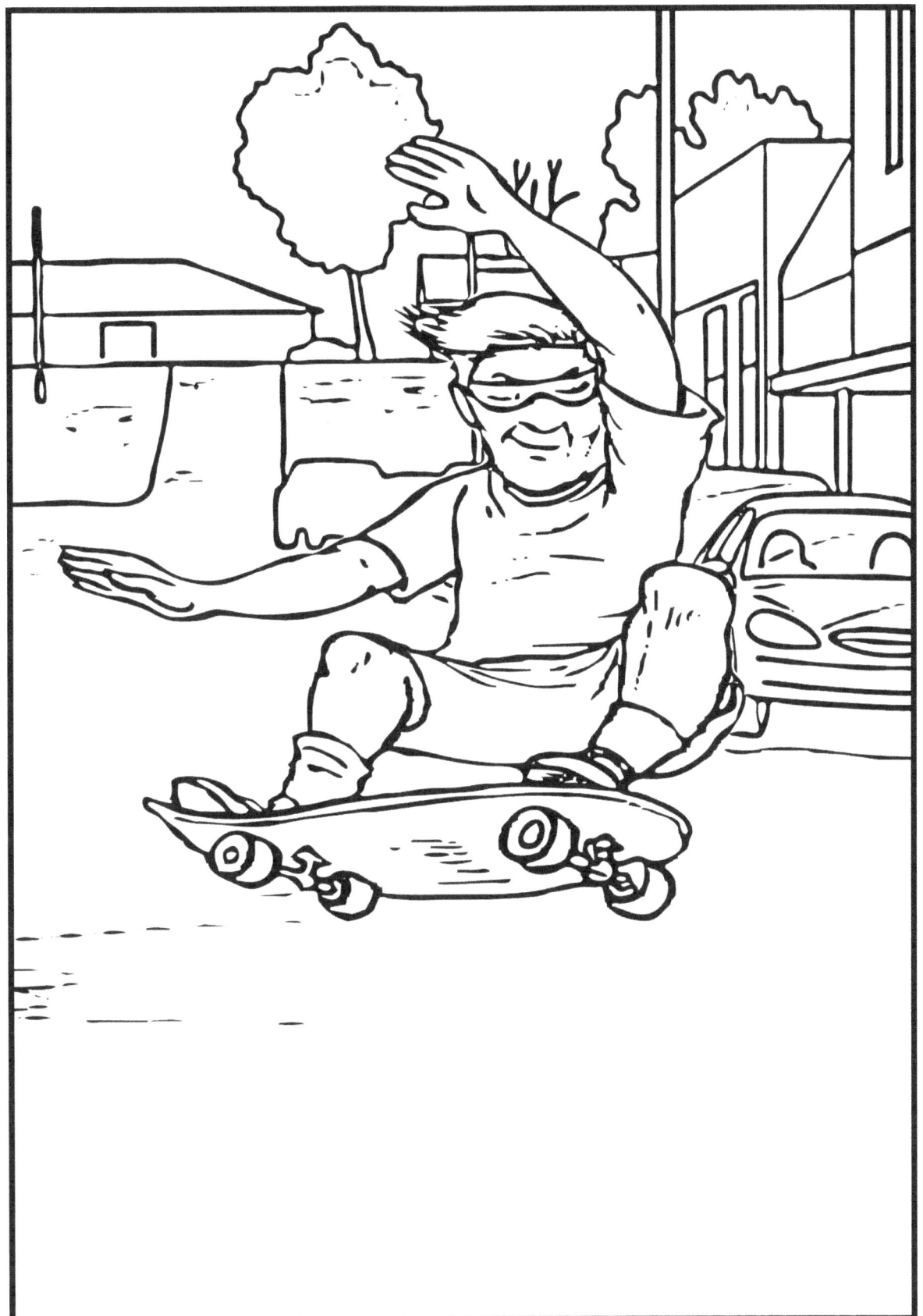

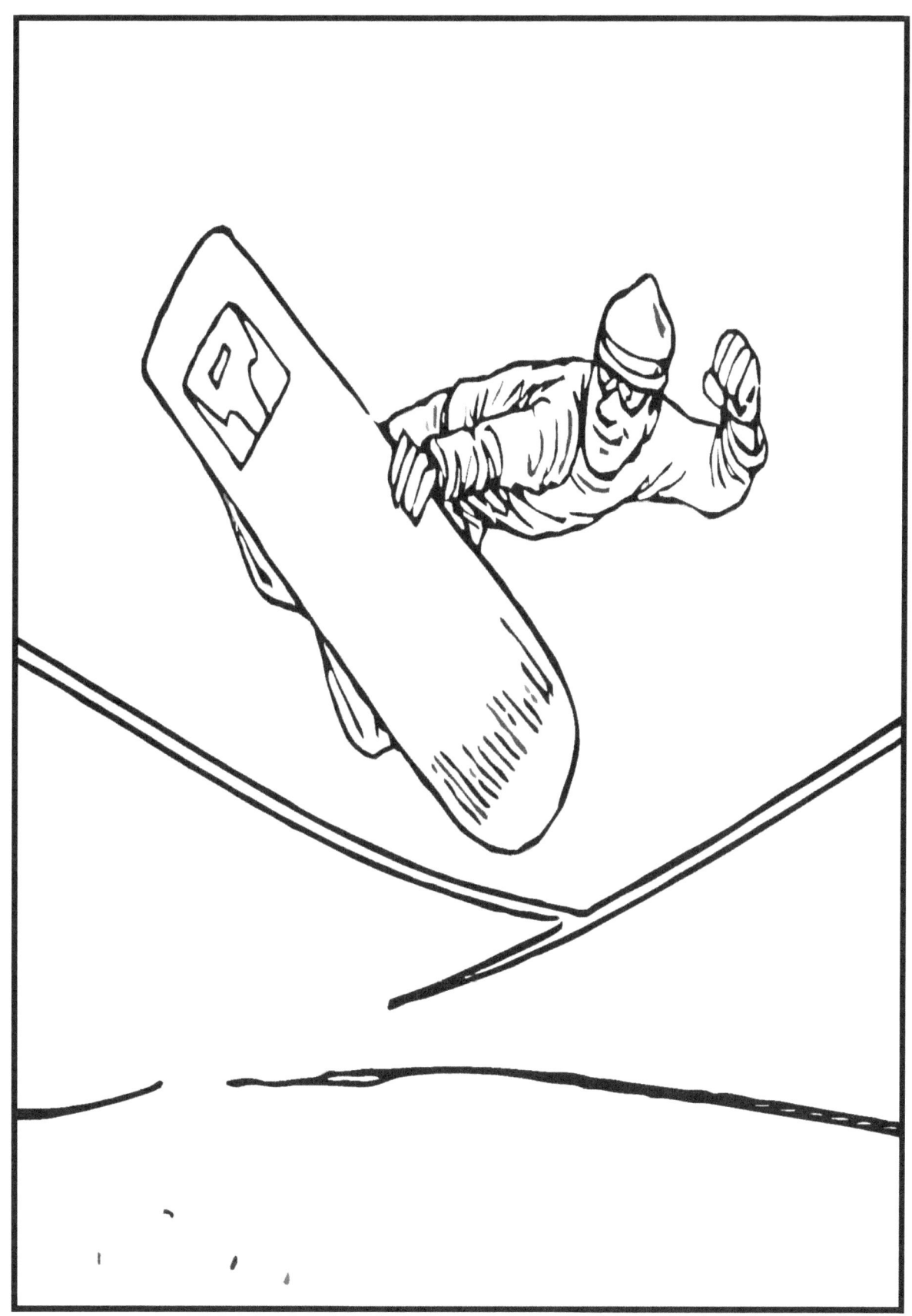

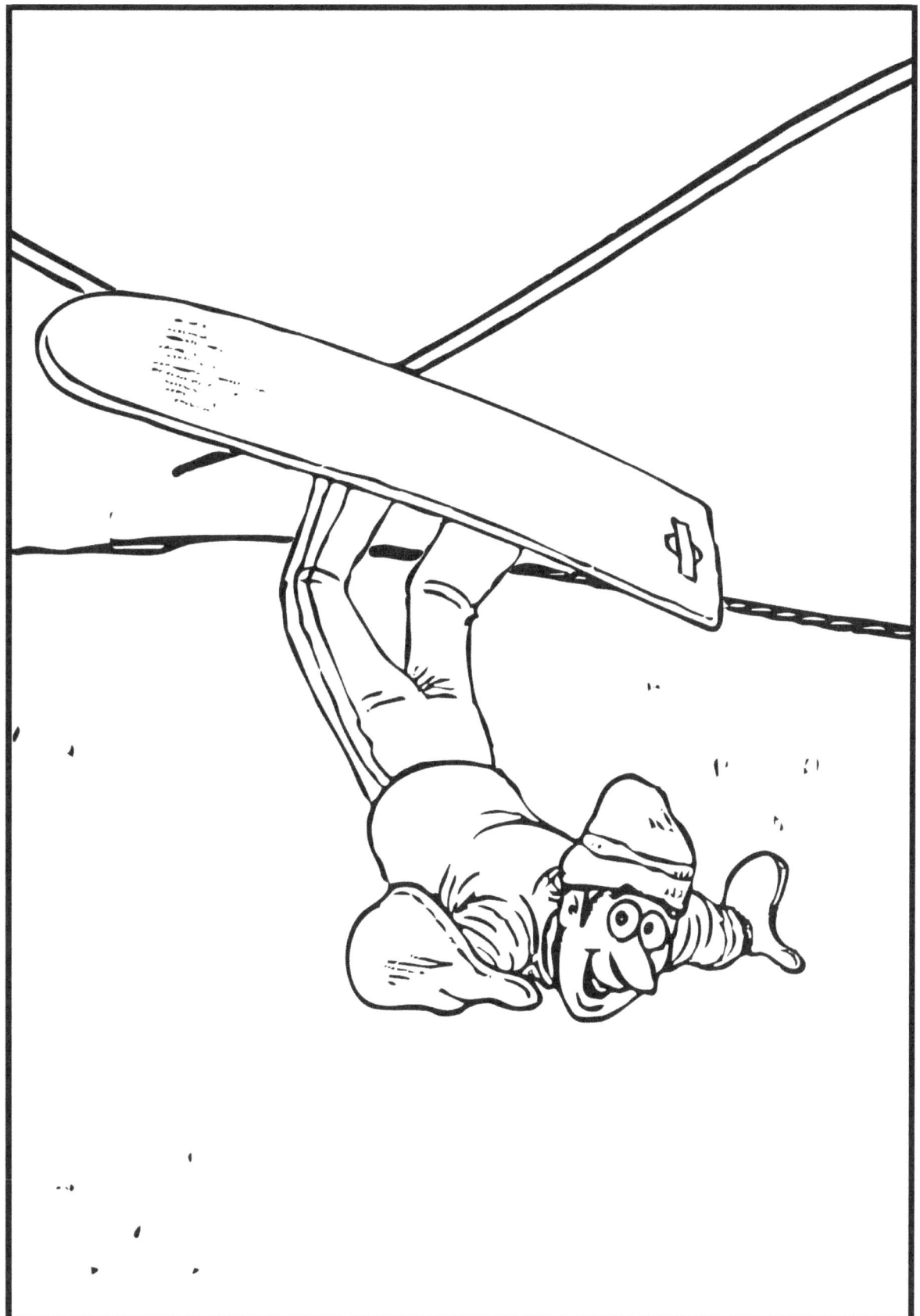

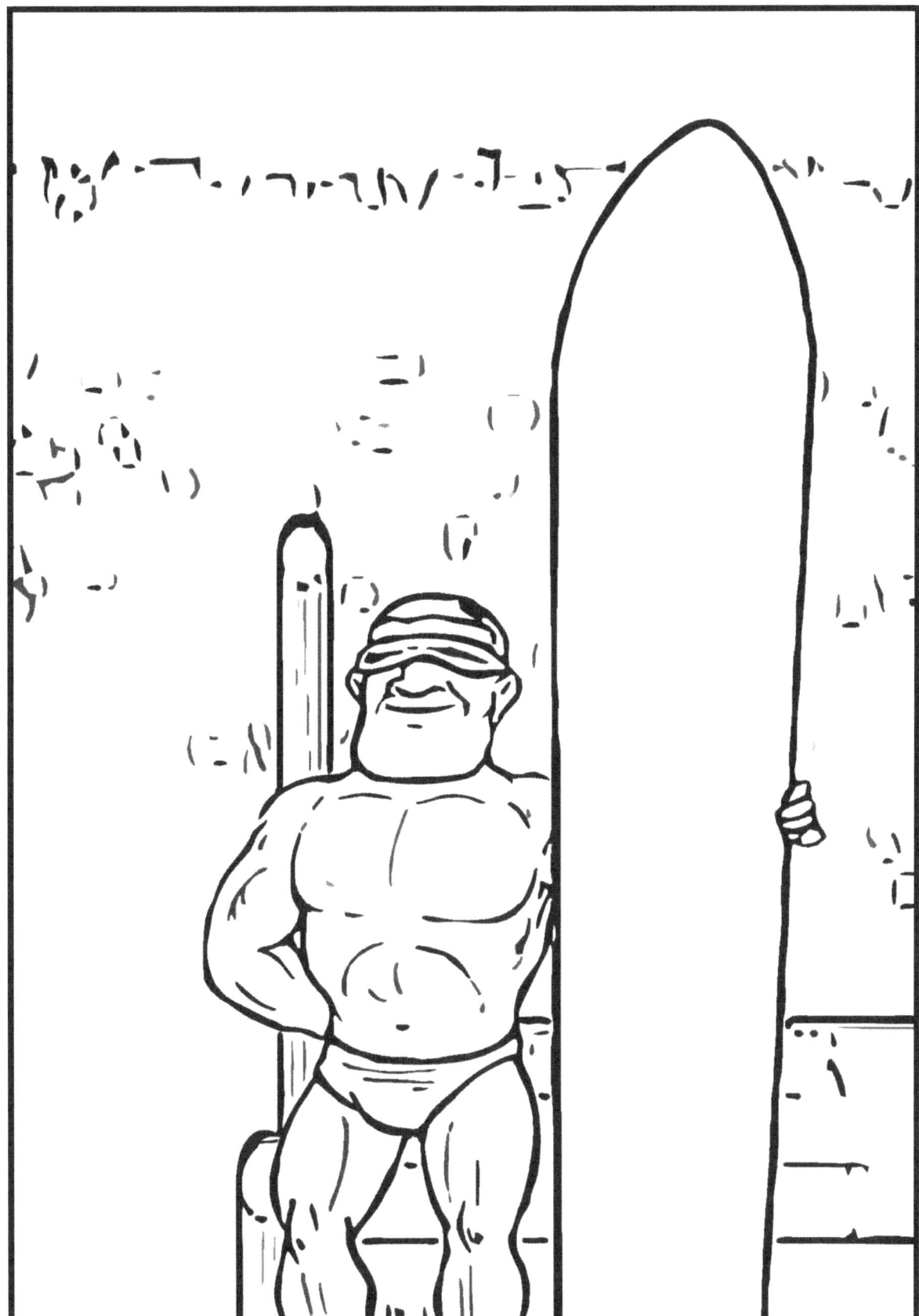

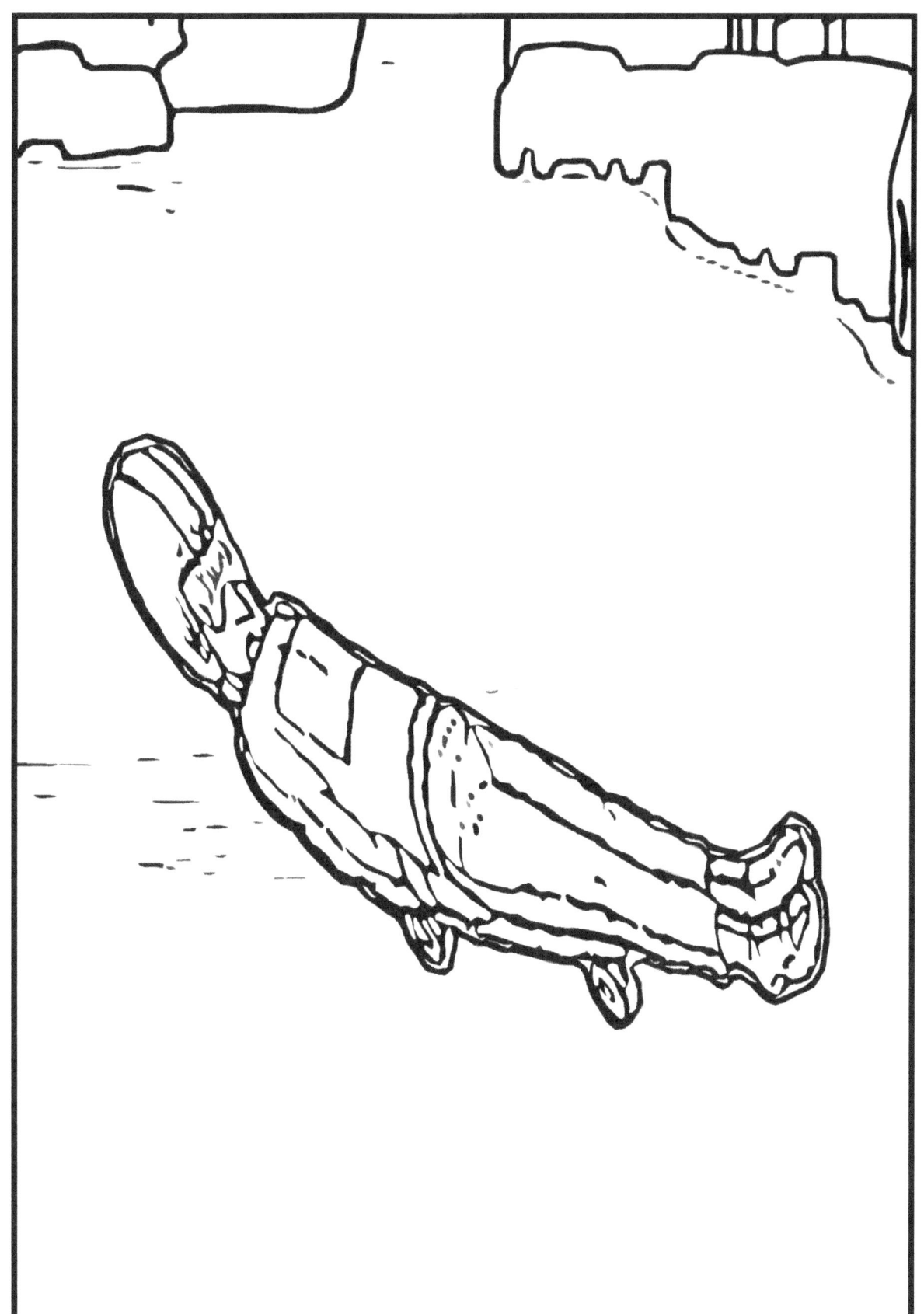

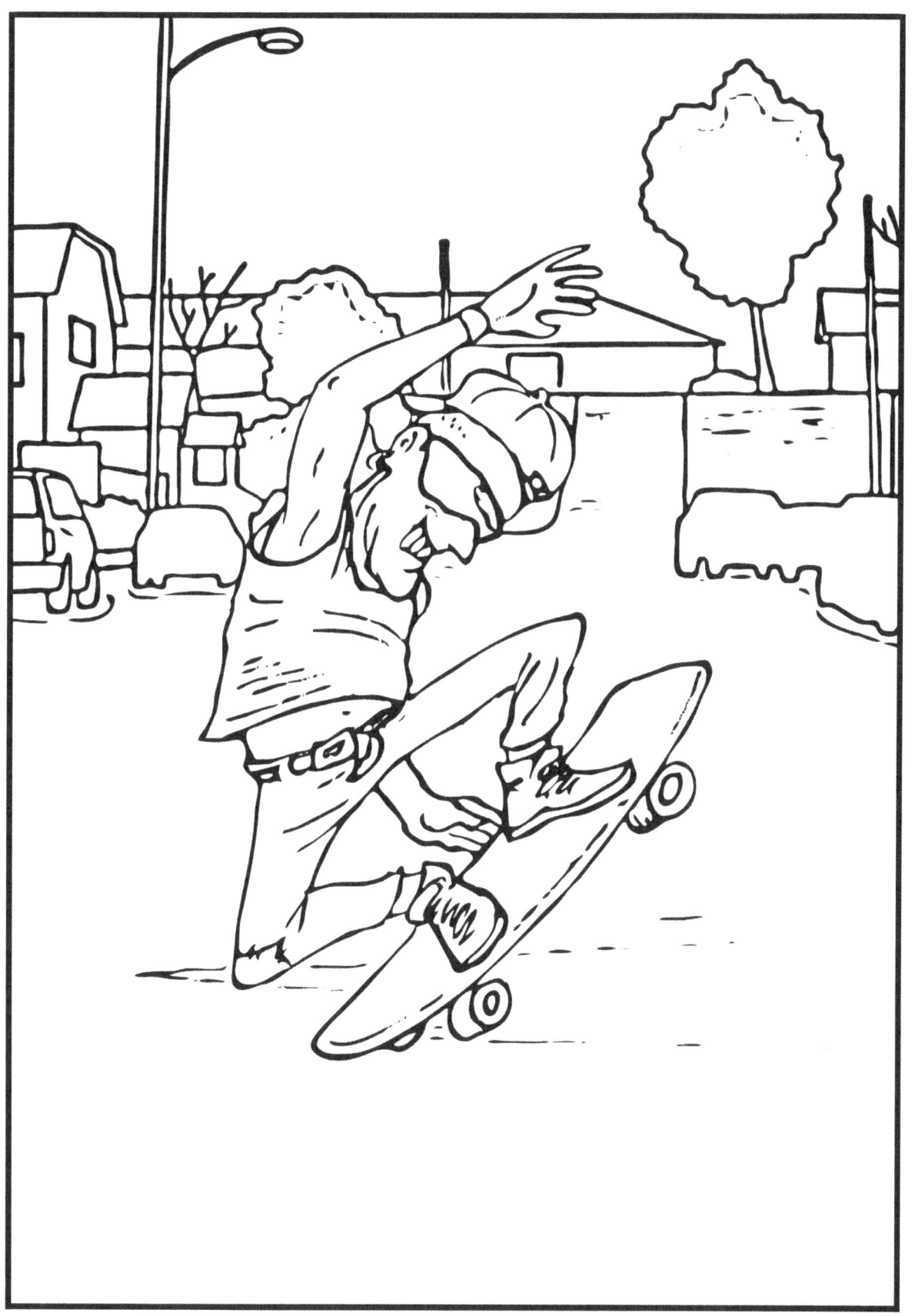

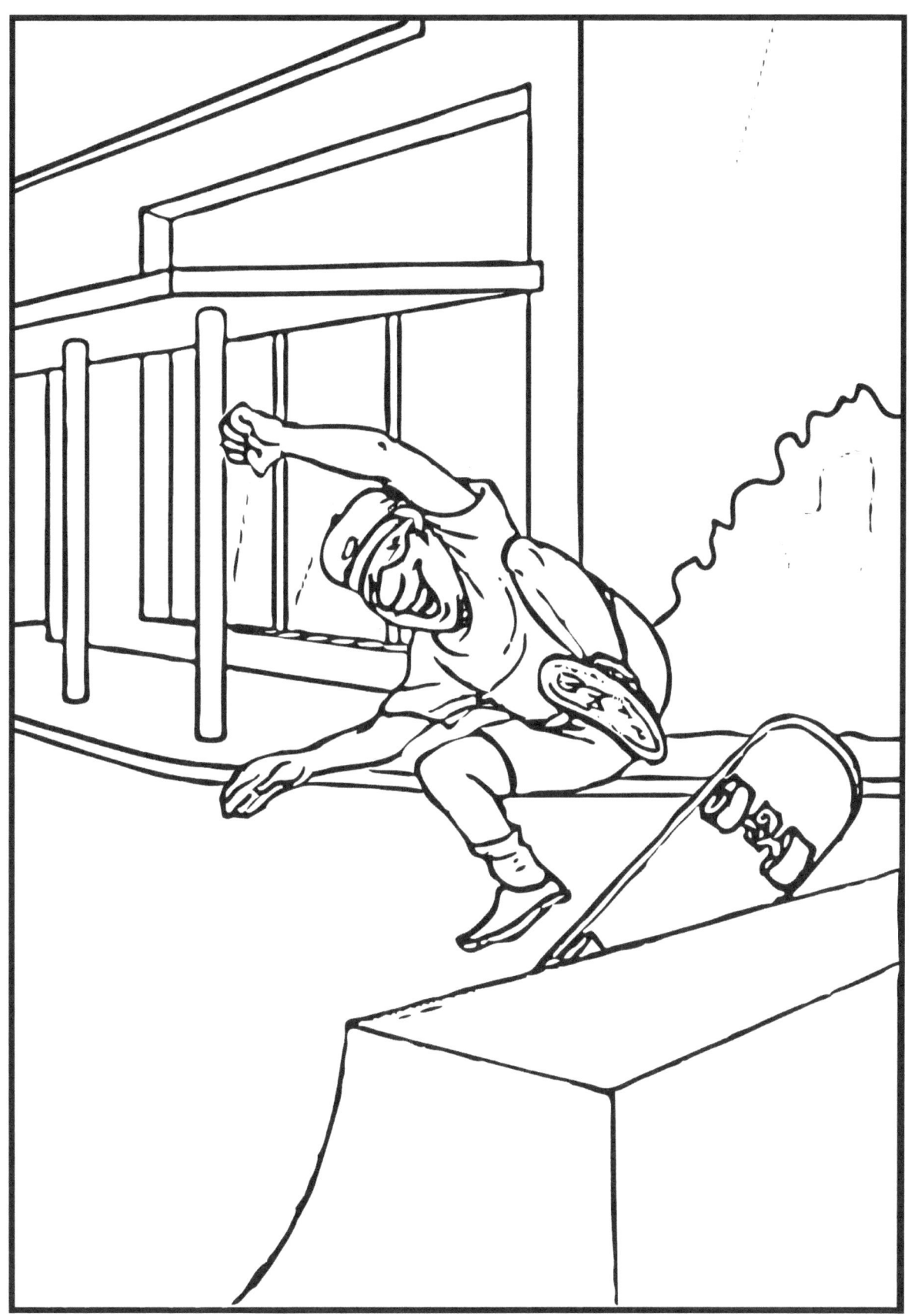

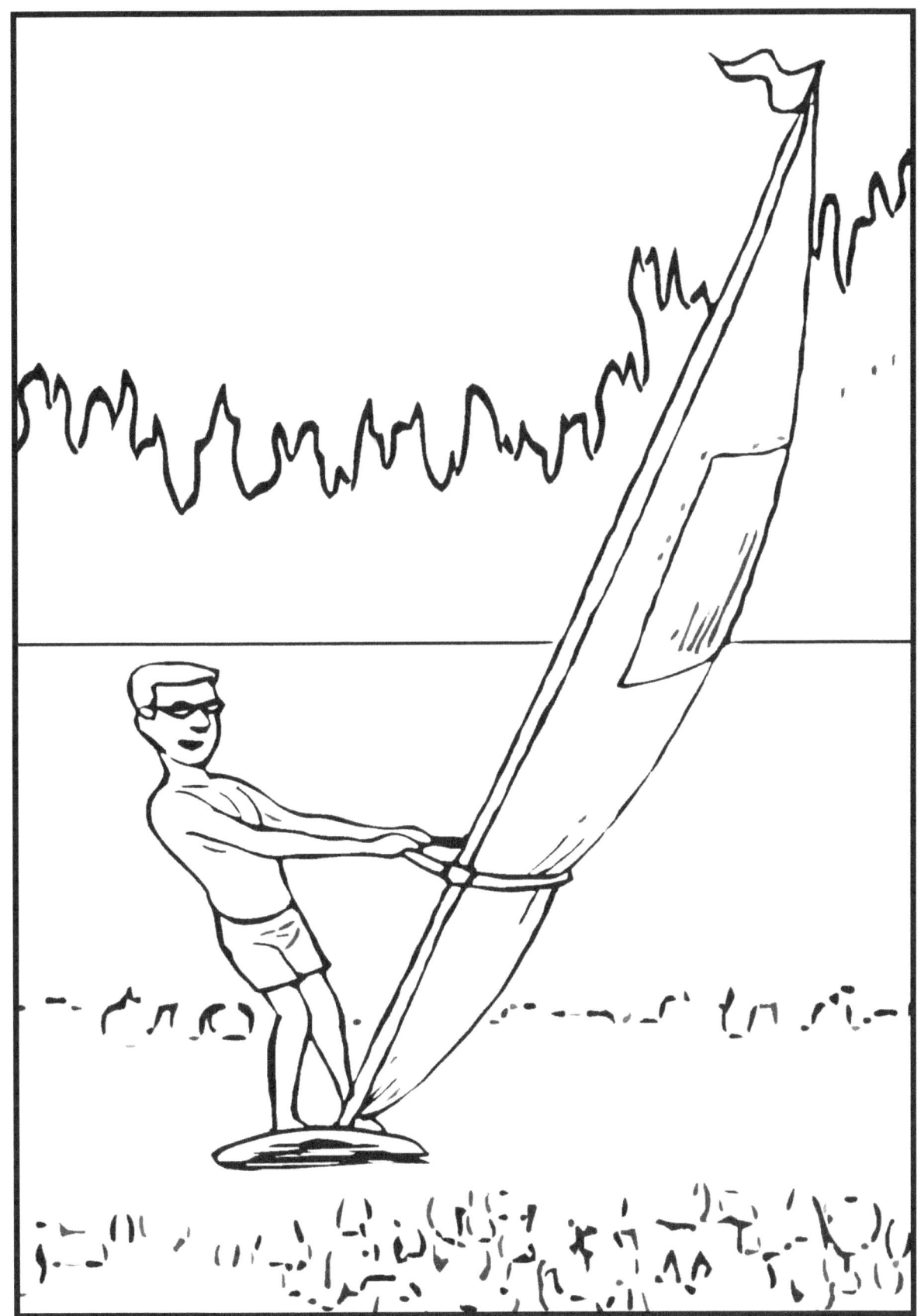

GIRLS playing SPORTS

Coloring Book

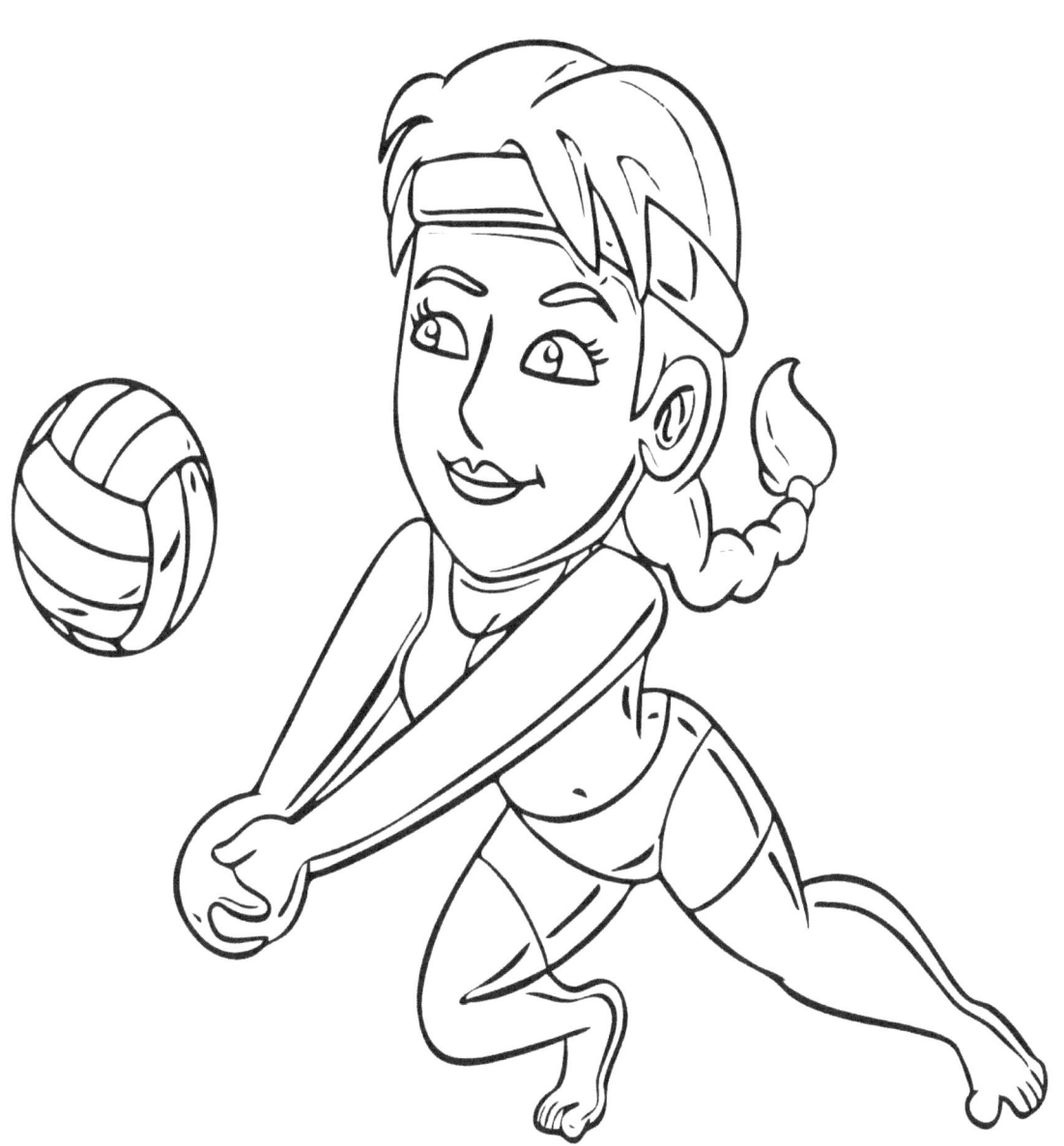

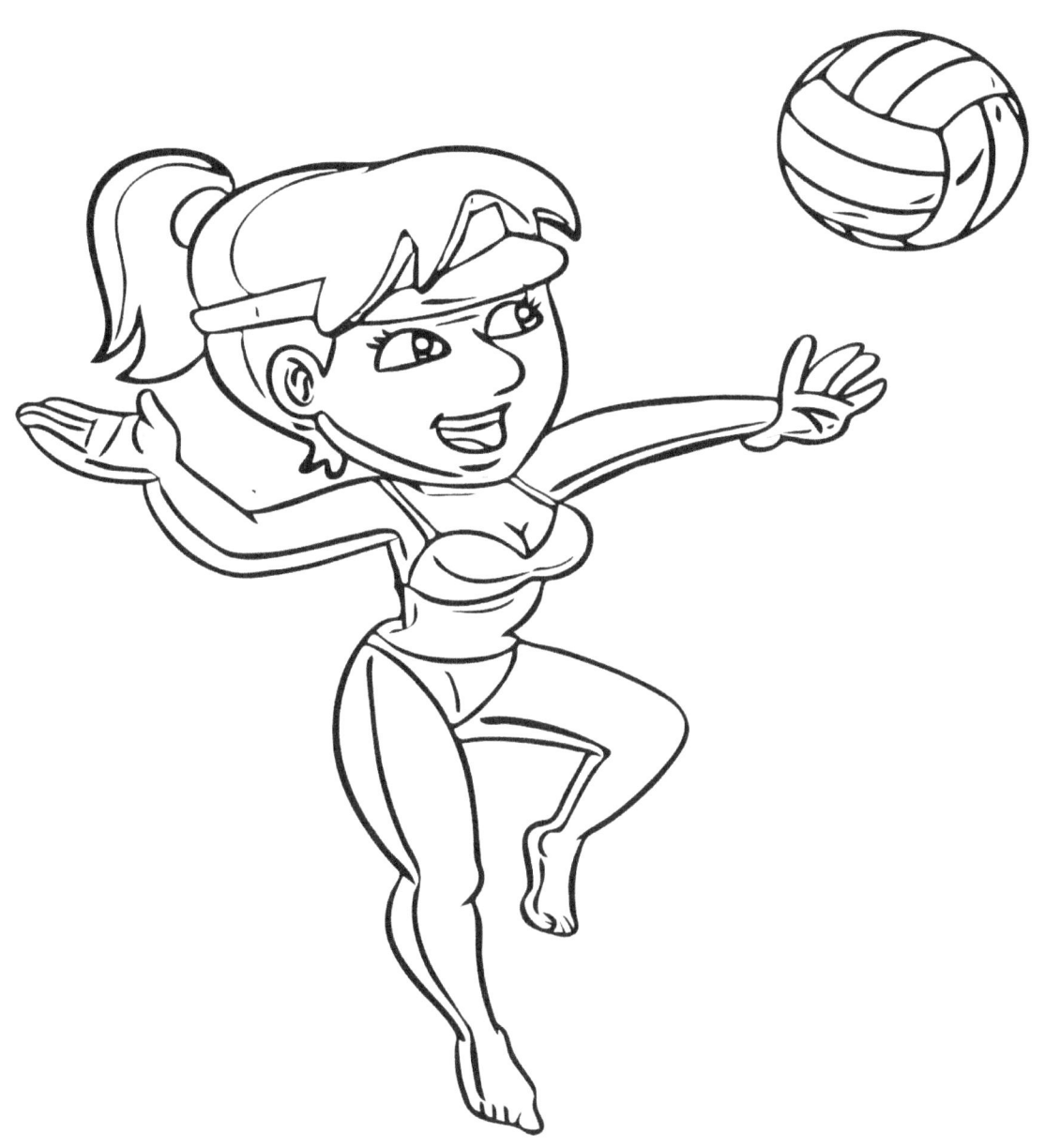

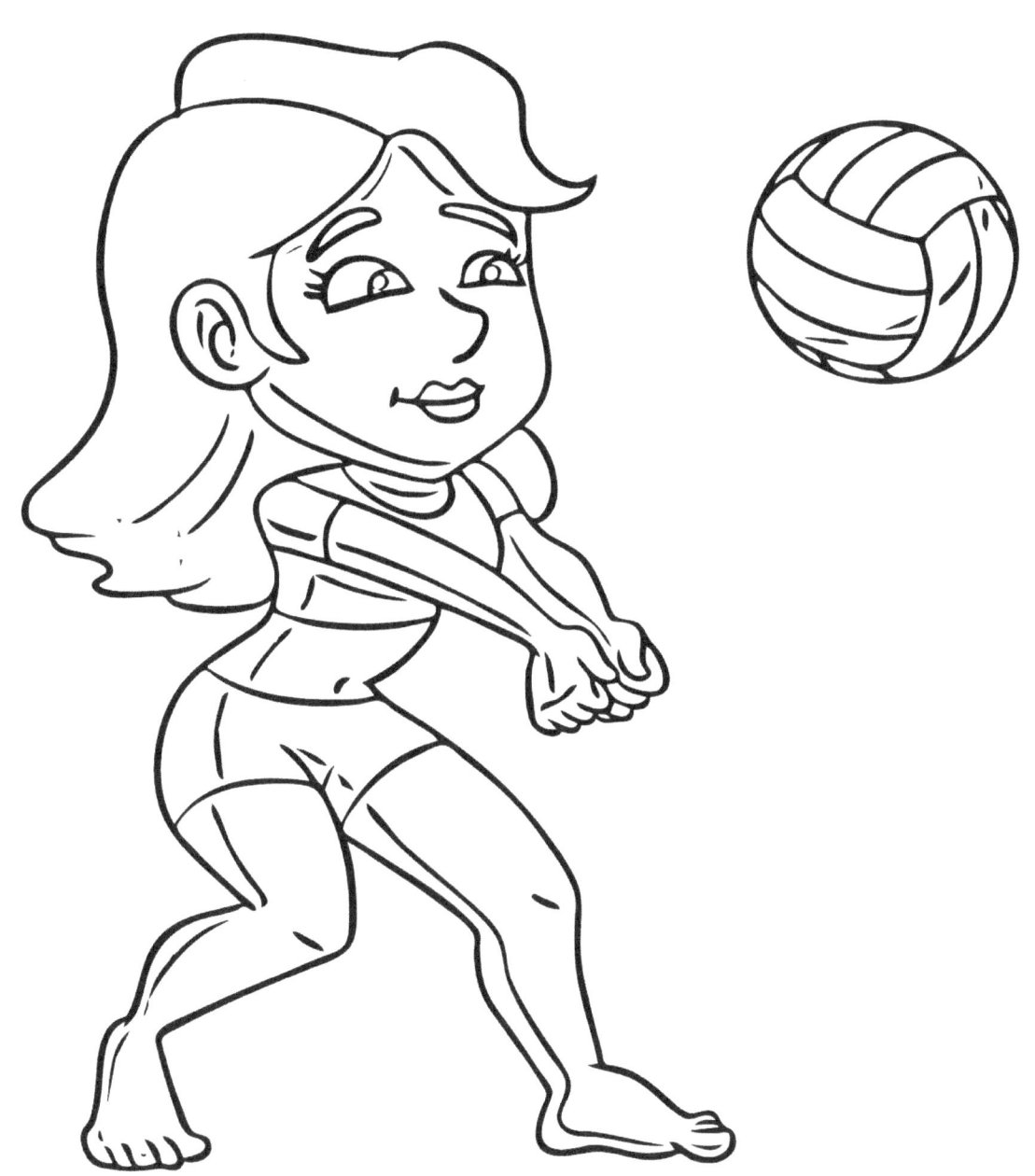

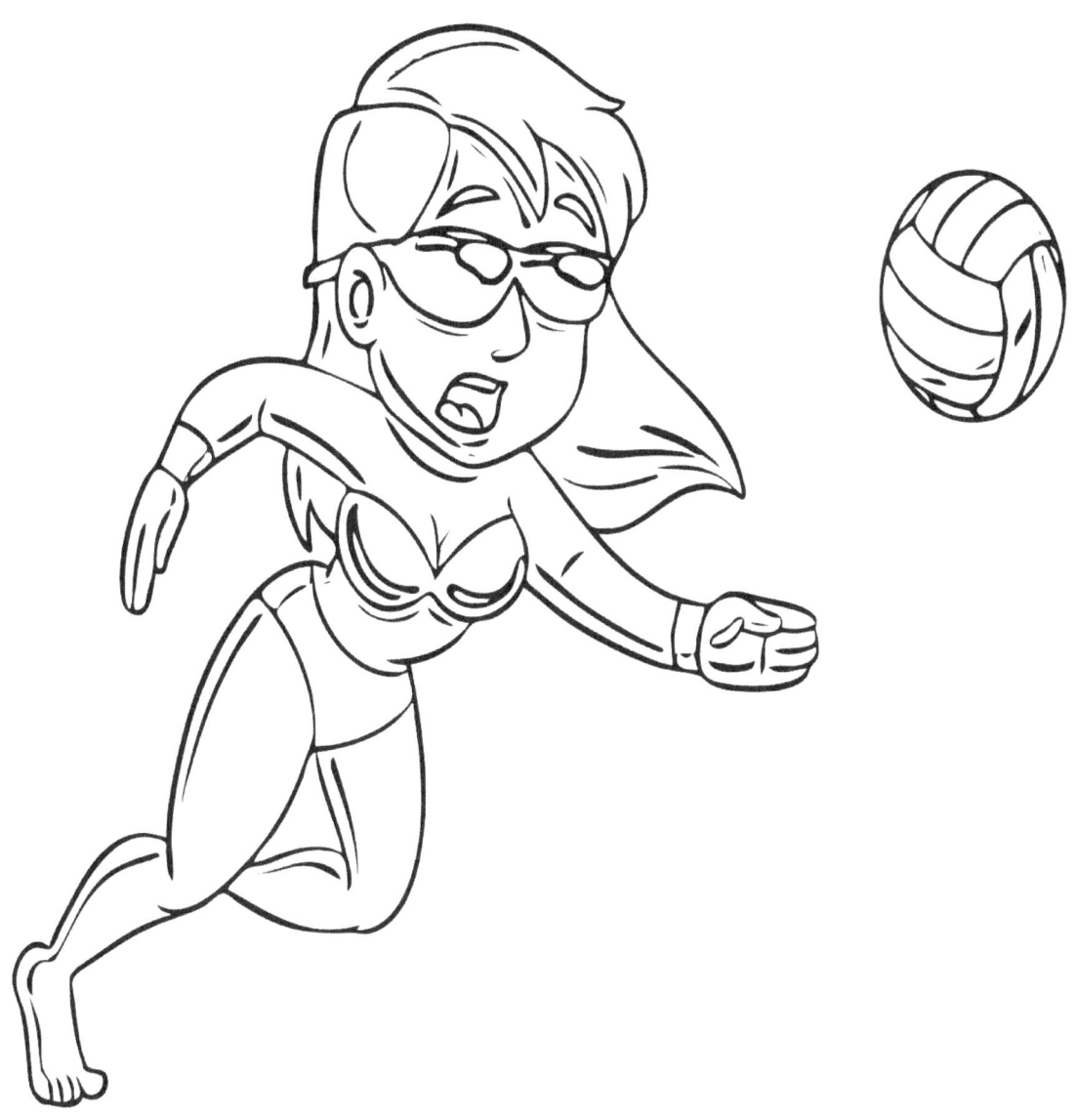

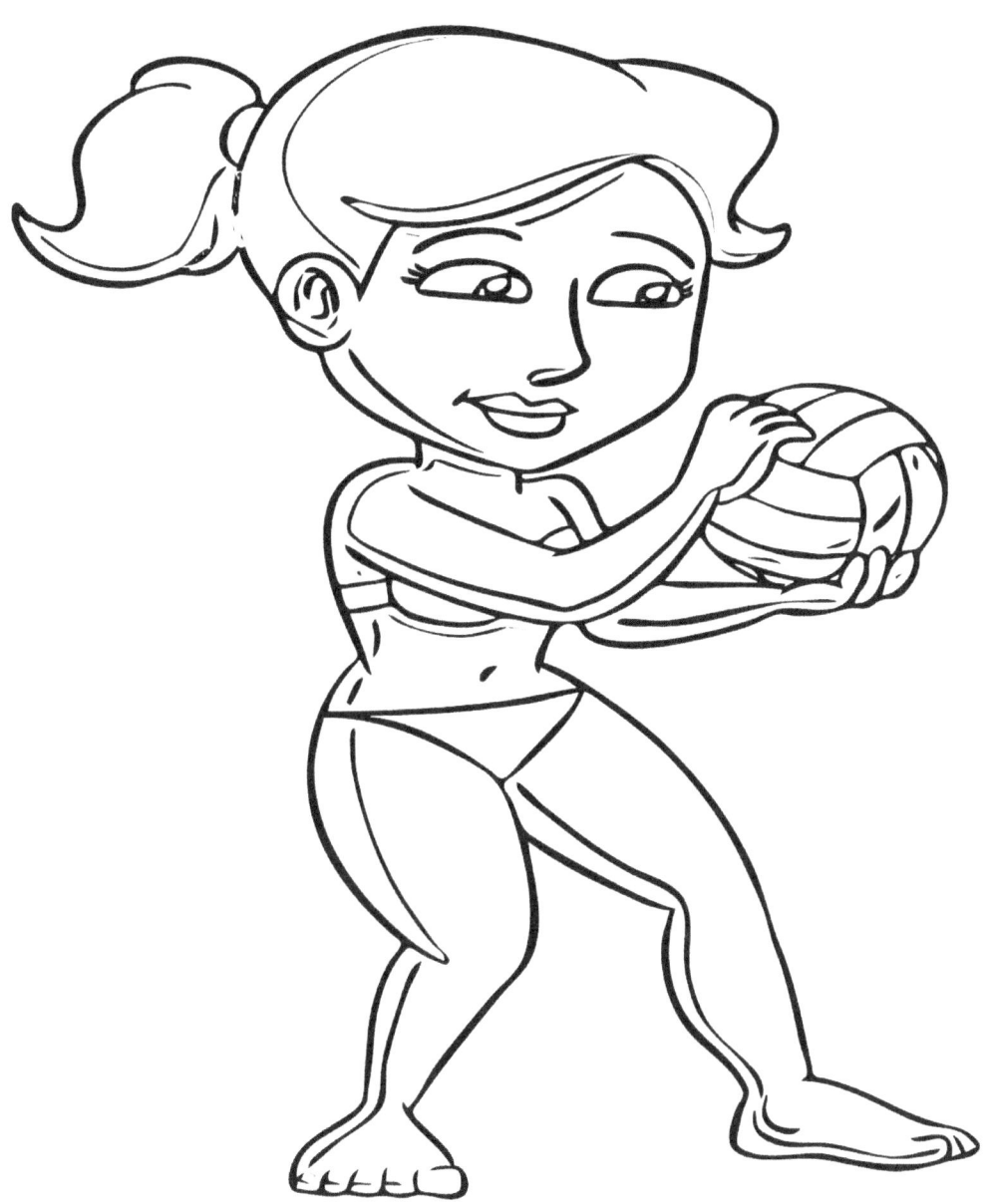

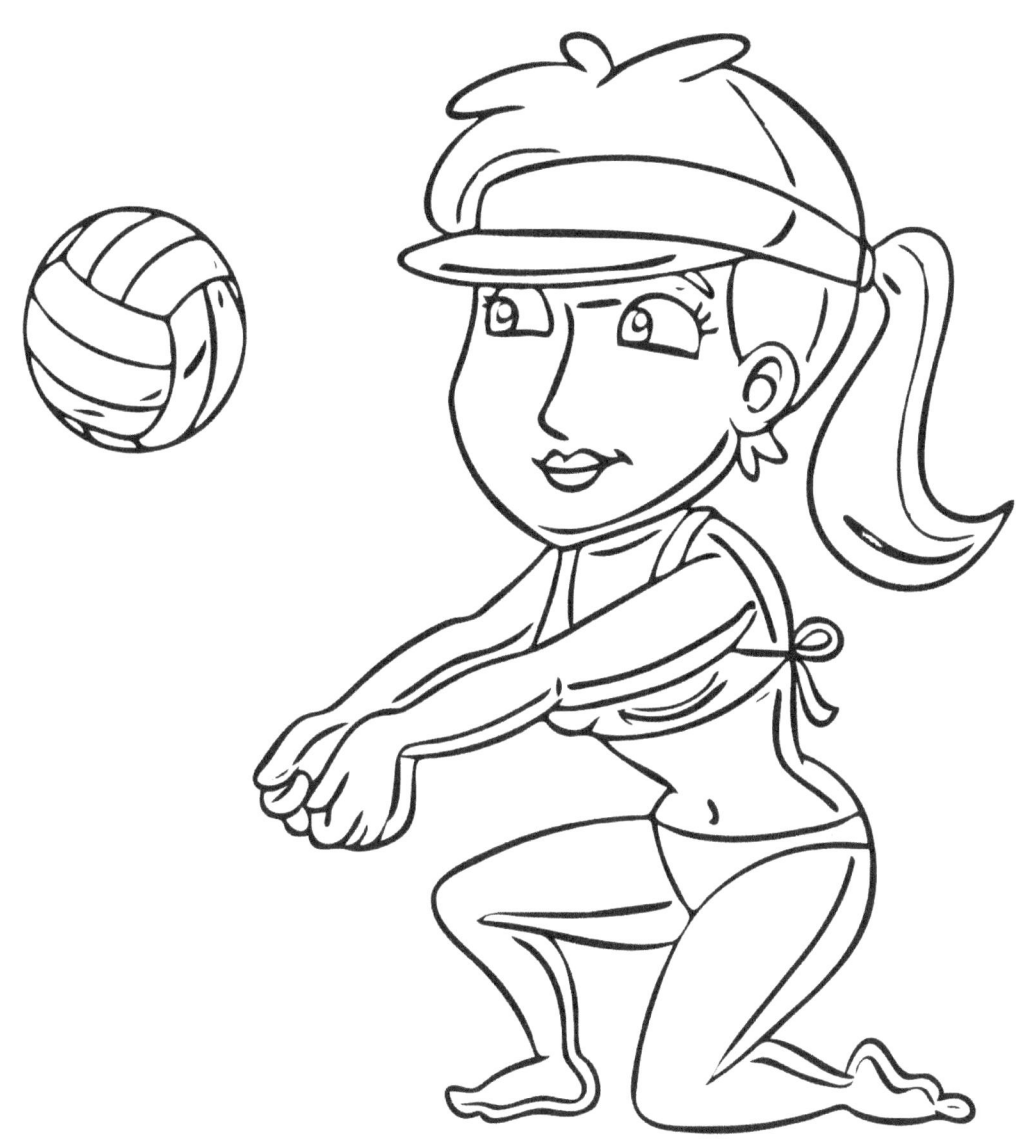

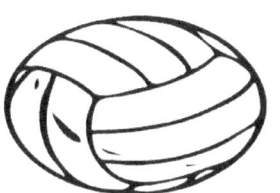
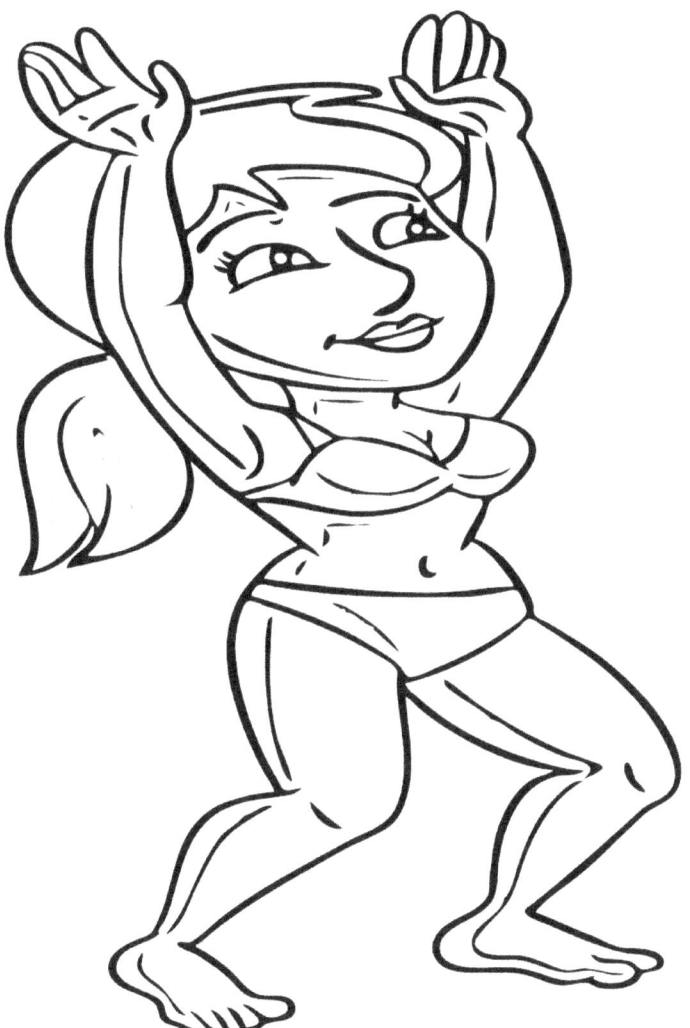

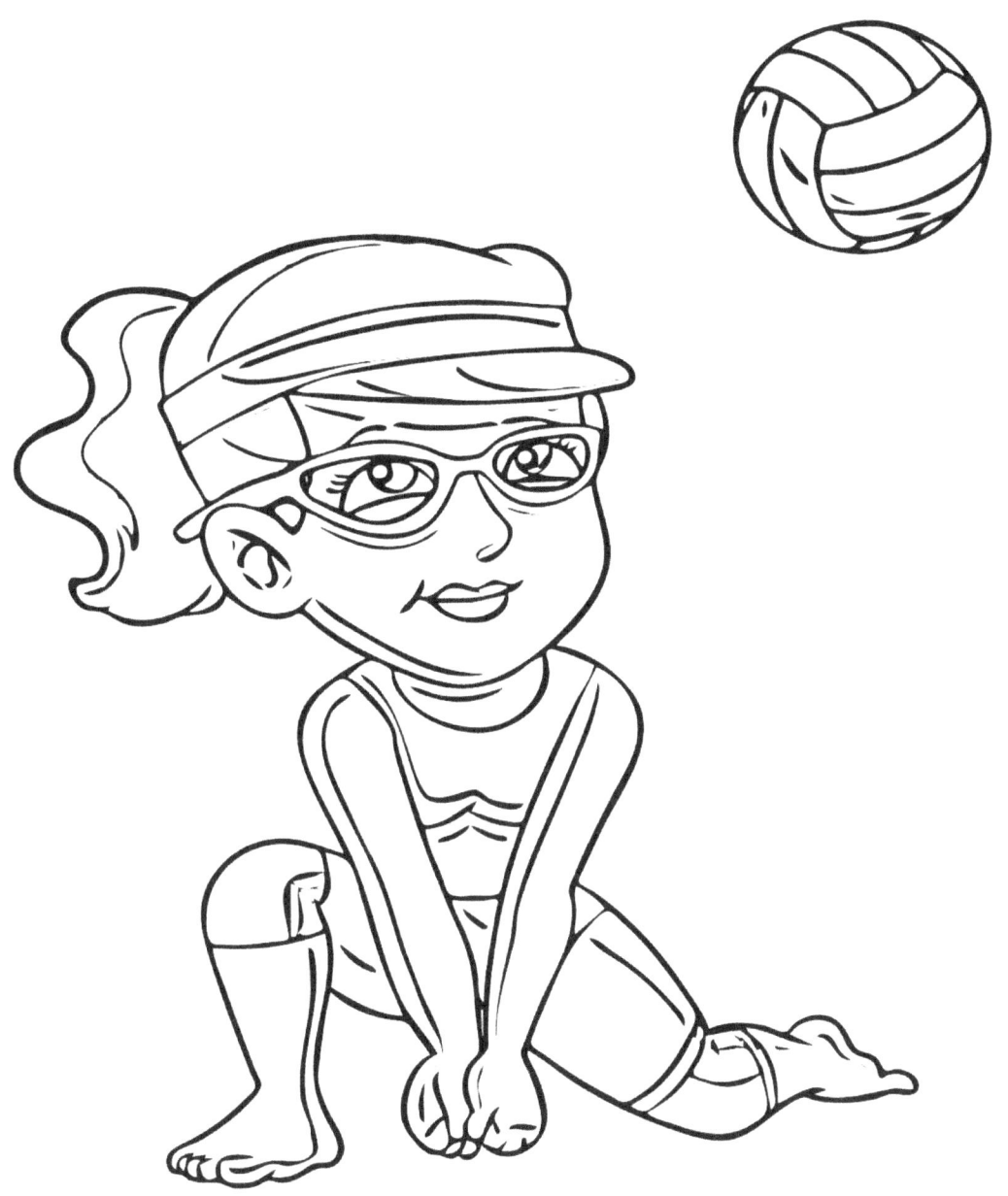

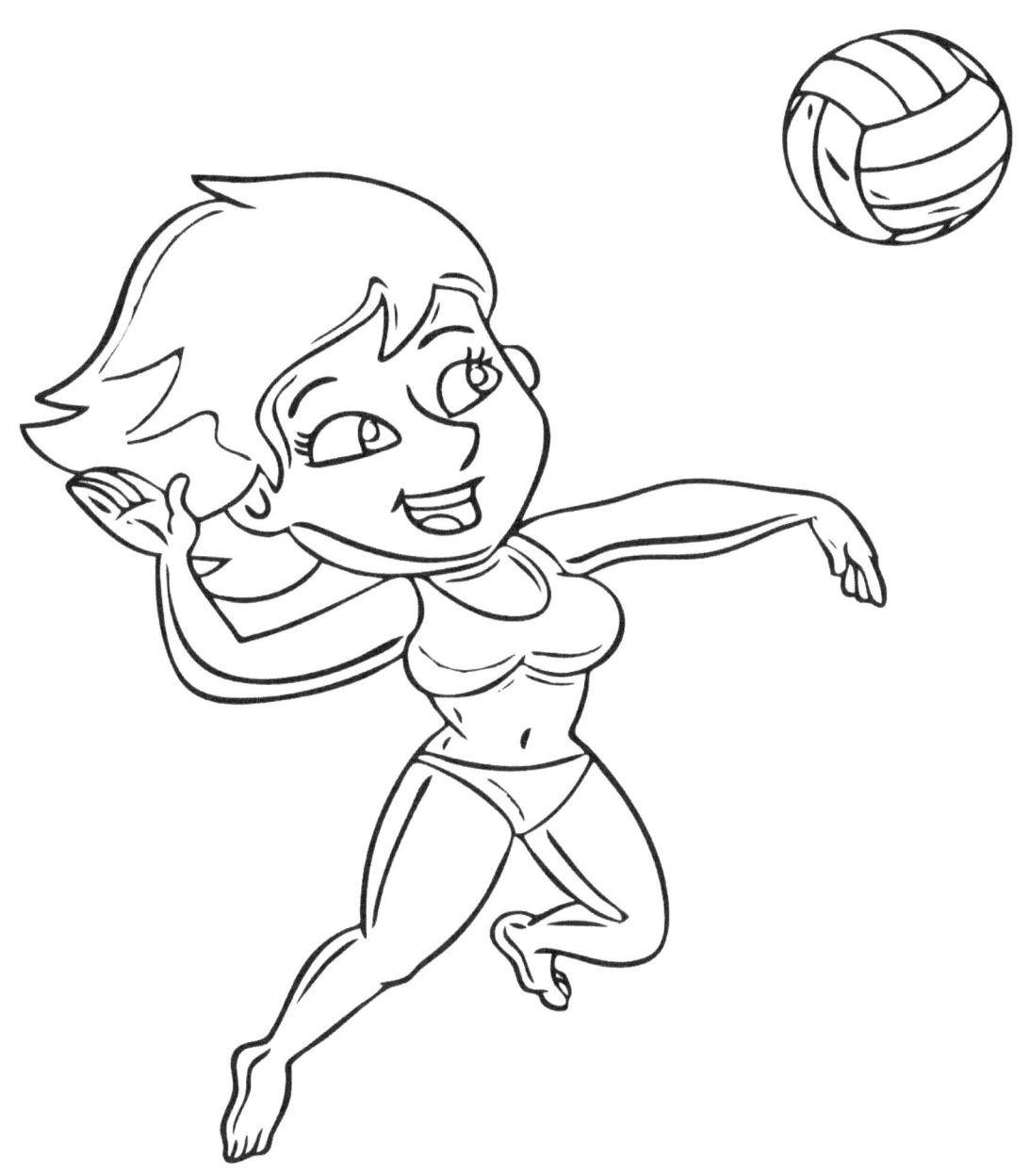

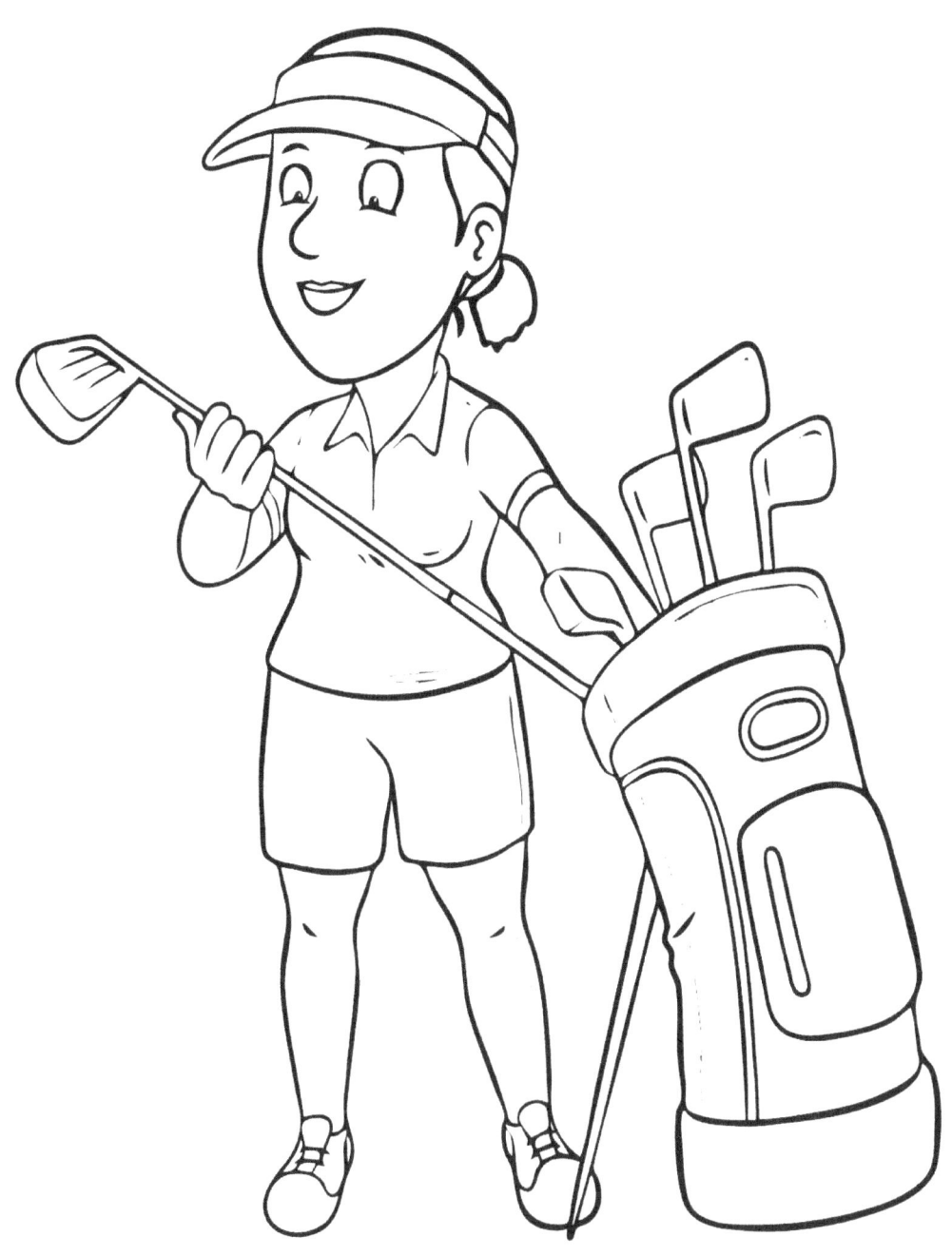

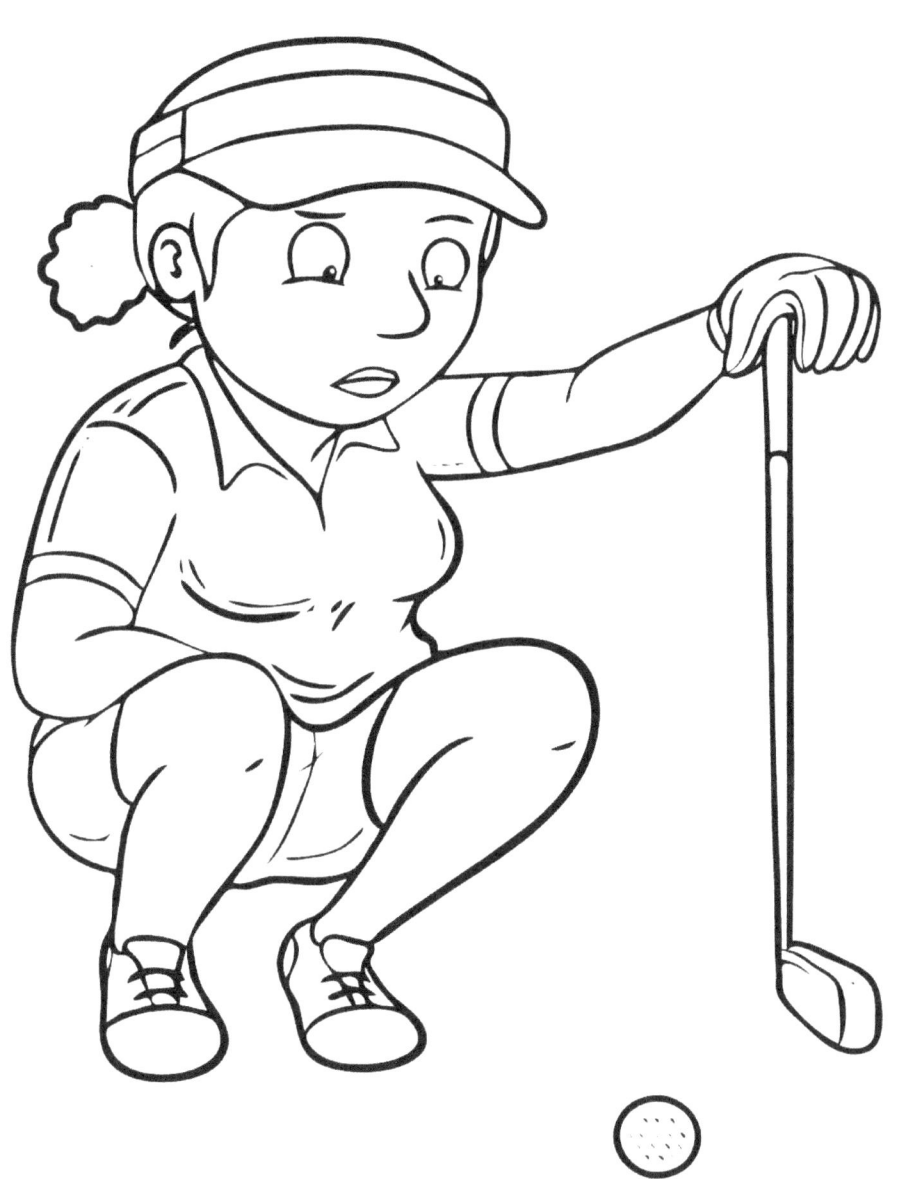

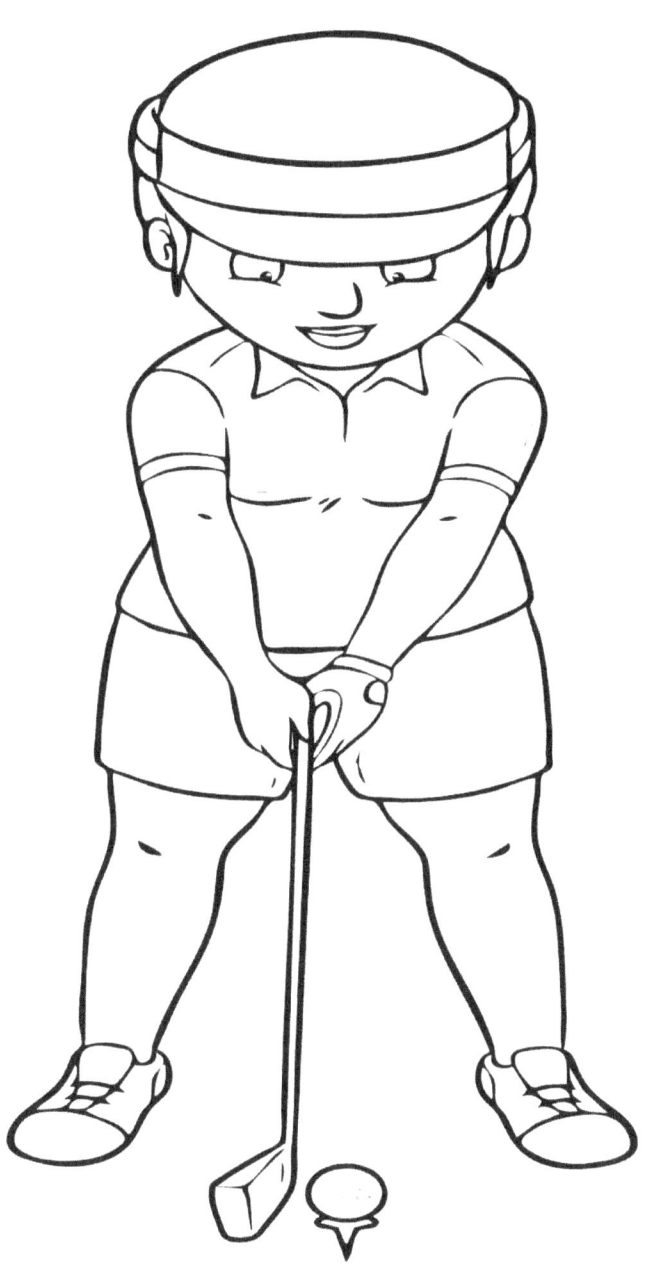

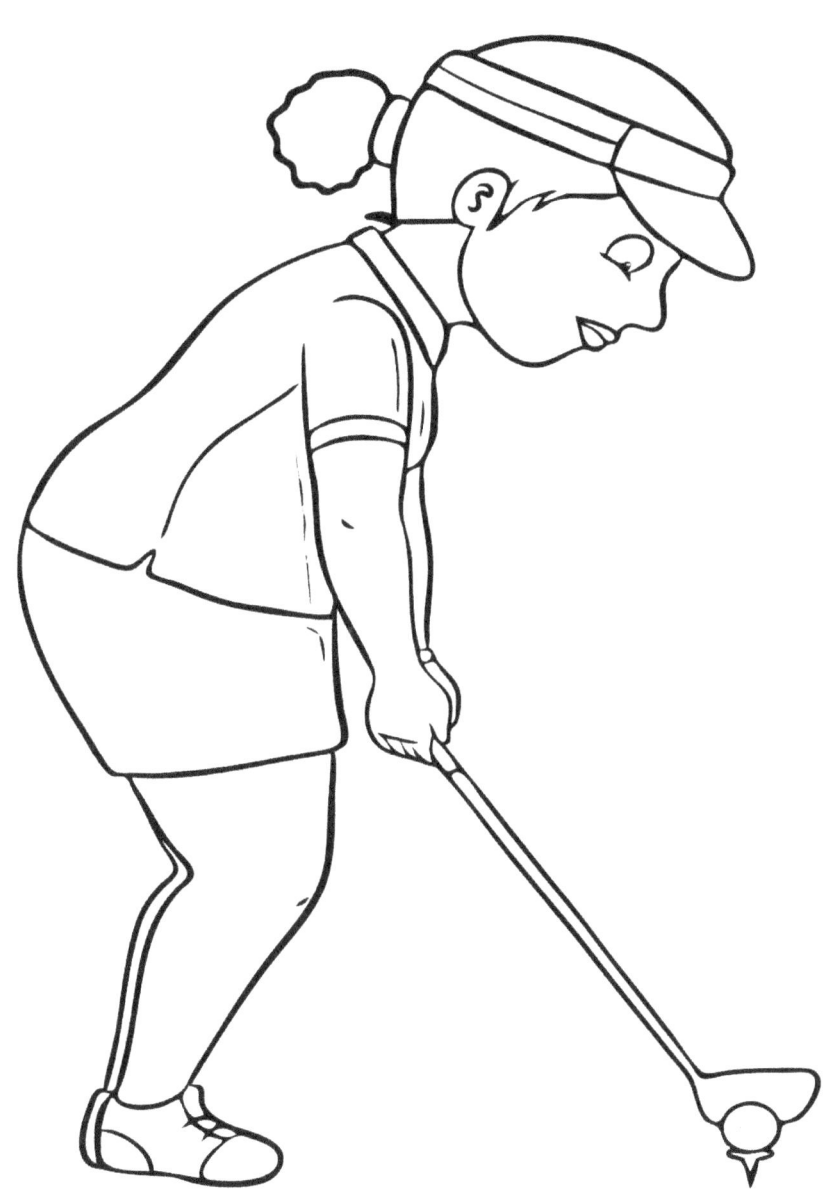

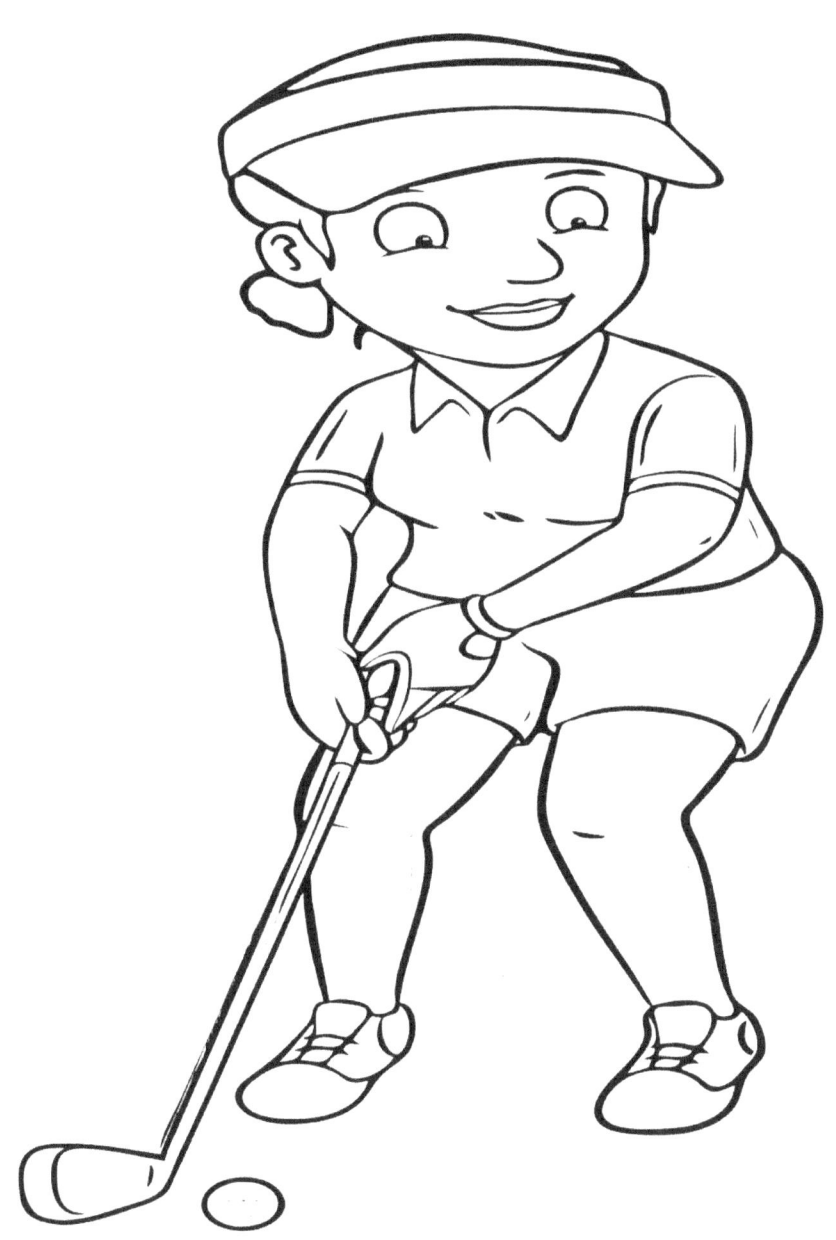

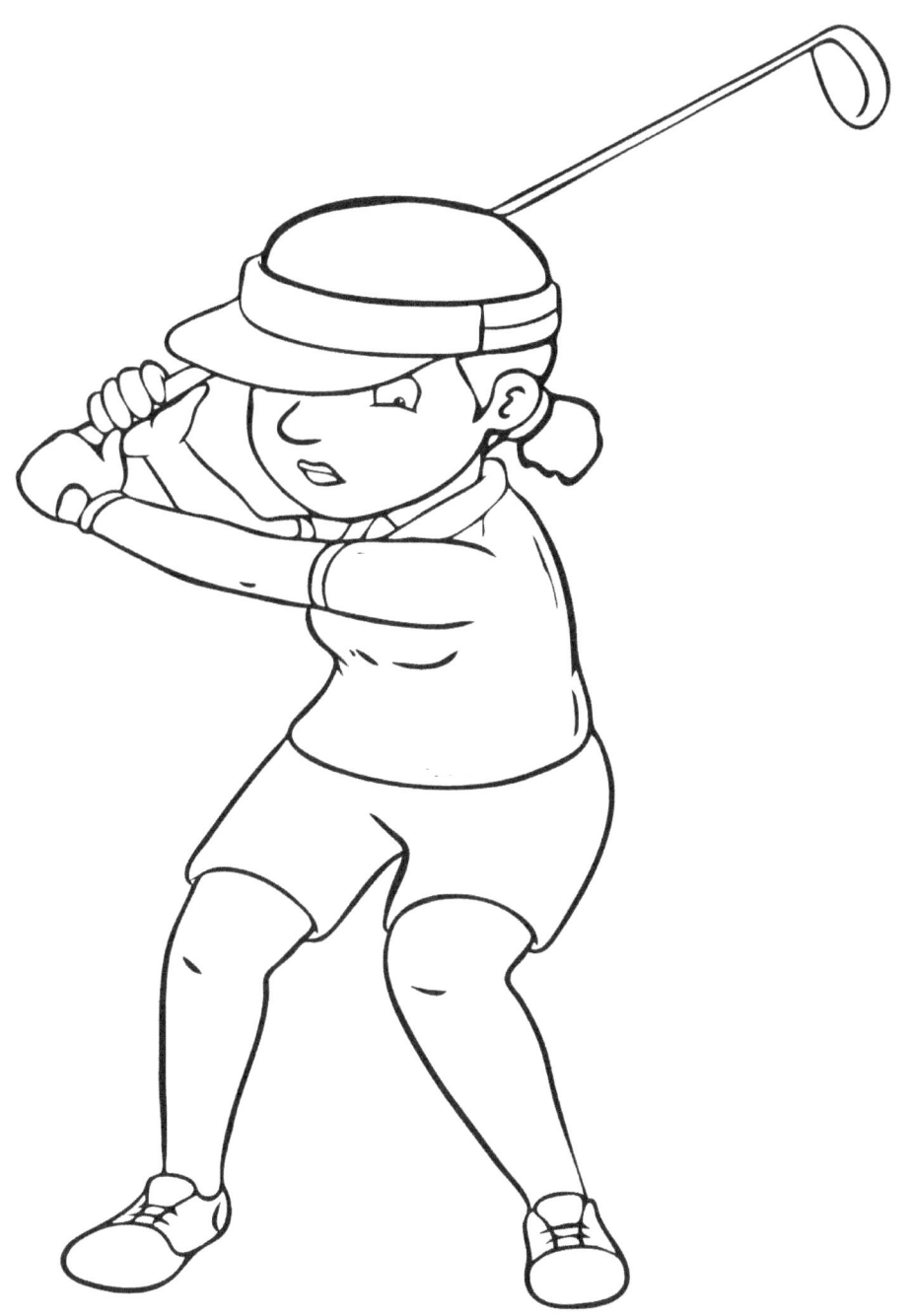

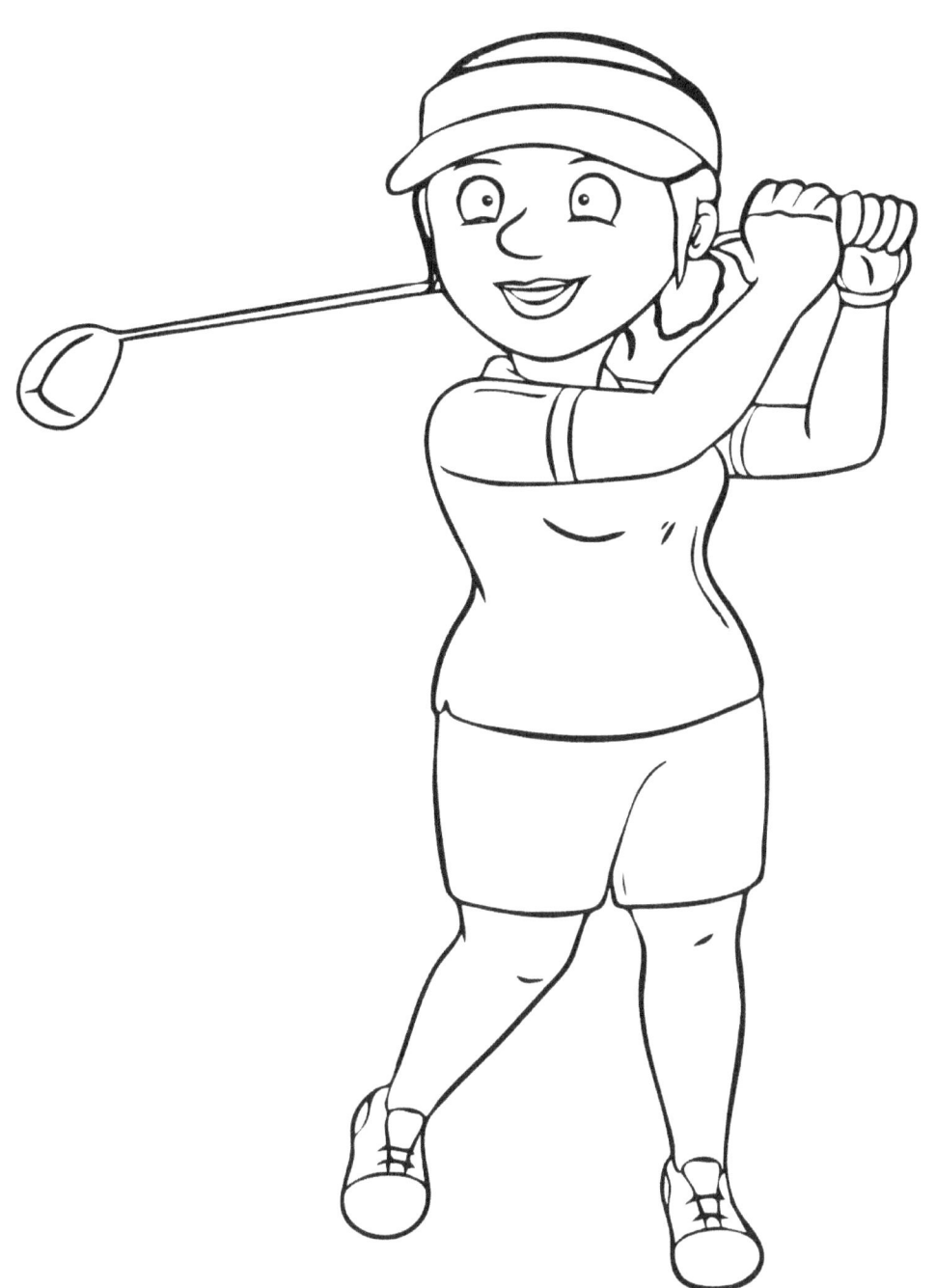

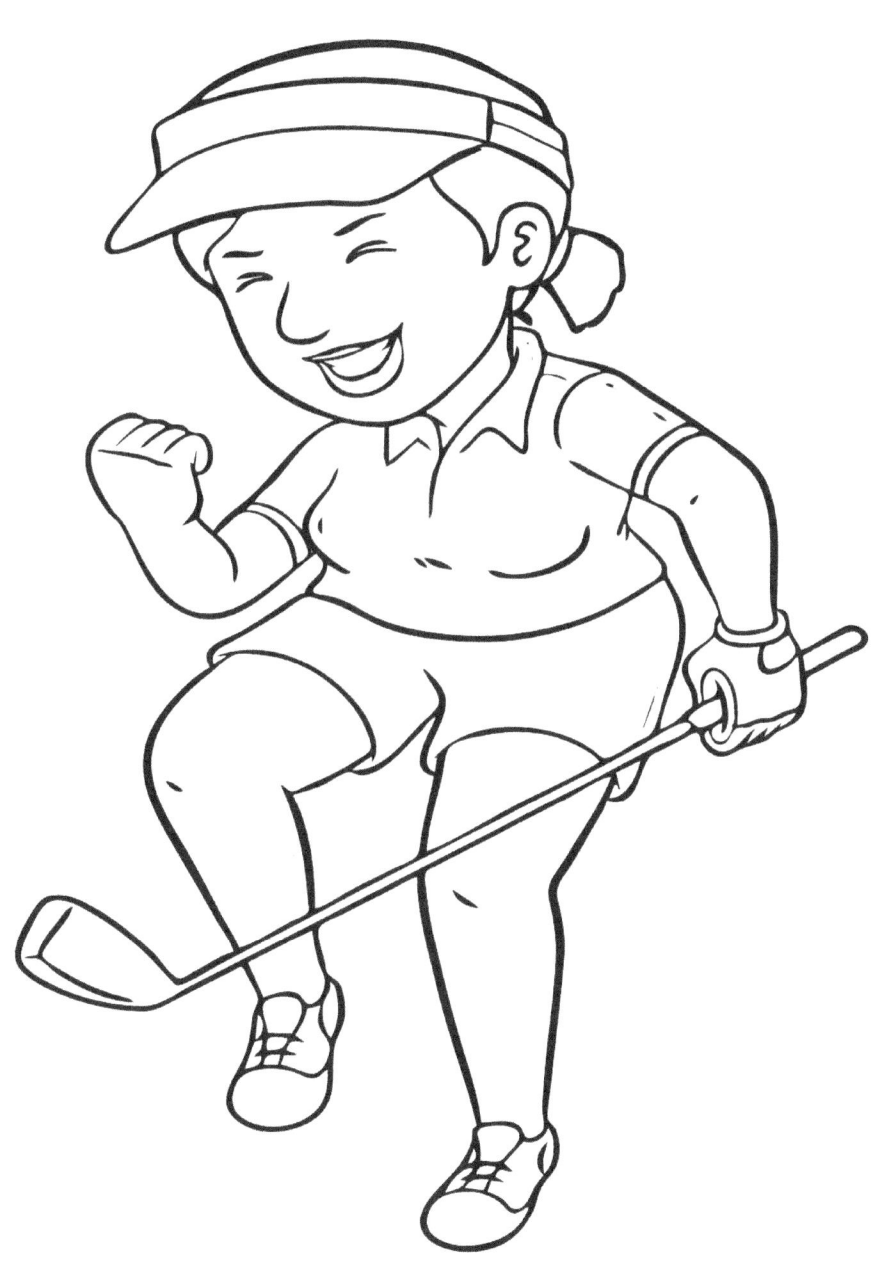

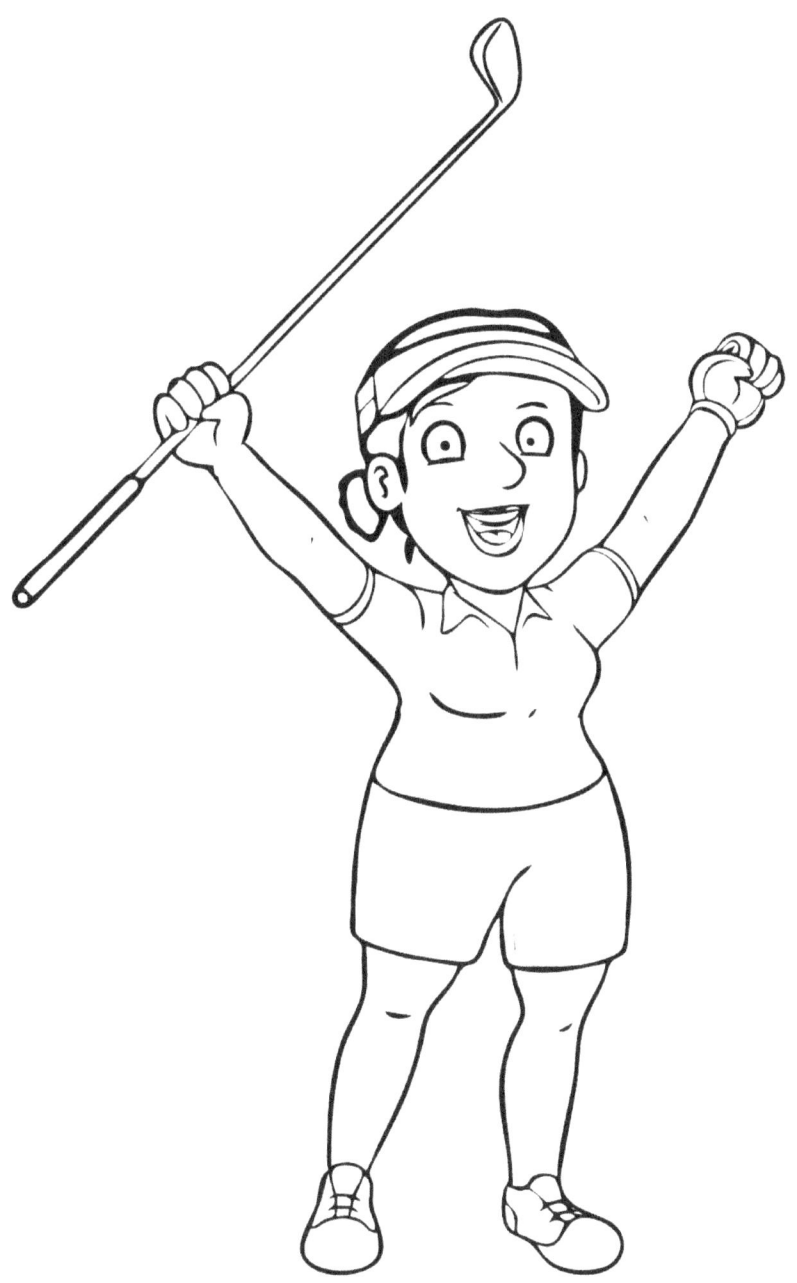

www.ingramcontent.com/pod-product-compliance
Lightning Source LLC
Chambersburg PA
CBHW060011210526
45170CB00017B/2289